THE
ANCIENT
Path

Understanding Your Journey
from Creation to Creator

JOSHUA M. JOST

DESTINY IMAGE EUROPE™ srl
Via Maiella, 1
66020 San Giovanni Teatino (Ch) - Italy

"Changing the world, one book at a time."

This book and all other Destiny Image Europe™ books are available at Christian bookstores and distributors worldwide.

To order products, or for any other correspondence:

DESTINY IMAGE EUROPE™ srl
Via Acquacorrente, 6
65123 - Pescara - Italy
Tel. +39 085 4716623 - Fax: +39 085 4716622
E-mail: info@eurodestinyimage.com

Or reach us on the Internet: **www.eurodestinyimage.com**

ISBN 13: 978-88-89127-28-5

For Worldwide Distribution, Printed in the U.S.A.

1 2 3 4 5 6 7 8 / 12 11 10 09 08 07

Endorsements

We desperately need the true power of God in the body of Christ today, not just a form of godliness that is devoid of it. Our worship and teaching are empty if they cannot change lives and overcome death.

It has been said that time proves the character and substantive depth of a person. Time has proven to me that Joshua Jost has a passion for God and the desire to make Him known.

The Ancient Path is a challenging, yet honest, look at the truth of God and what it really means to follow Him. For those willing to face its message, this book will reveal the road to a powerful and life-changing walk with God.

Dr. J. Doug Stringer,
Founder and President,
Turning Point Ministries International

The Ancient Path is a refreshing, thought provoking, spiritually inspiring book that makes you stop and really think about your faith and beliefs. As I read the book, a phrase came to mind about the author, "a philosopher of truth." As you compare your walk with the Lord with the journey outlined in the pages of *The Ancient Path*, you'll find Scripture coming to life through its poetic descriptions and intimate spiritual truths.

Kathleen Steele Tolleson
HIS Ministry International

Table of Contents

Introduction

You are about to begin a journey. May you enjoy the vistas, the beauty, and the challenge. May you find the chapter breaks as park benches along the path, places to stop and reflect upon your travels. In the end may you find yourself changed more by the journey itself than by the destination.

Why Read This Book?

I asked myself many times: *Why write this book?* Will anyone want to read what I have to say, what I have sought after, and what I have discovered? When millions of books line the shelves of retail booksellers and the warehouses of Amazon, what difference will one more make? Why would anyone want to pick up this one little insignificant work?

A thousand "whys" have been asked as I poured my thoughts onto paper—a thousand questions about God, who He is, why He does what He does—ever searching for deeper understanding, beyond the textbook answers, into the real heart of the Creator. I believe we start in blind faith, but we're not meant to stay there. I think that He wants us to endlessly pursue these revelations. It's as if He is standing on the top of a mountain, waiting for us to come and find Him so He can open up a whole new vista for us.

Discovering life's answers for yourself is more meaningful than reading textbook answers to generic questions.

Personal life-changing stories are woven throughout the Bible. Between "so-and-so begat so-and-so" blind eyes were healed, mothers cried, families celebrated, and armies battled—through amazing and subtle events people discovered God. These experiences carry us on the path to Heaven as we learn to understand the Father in the changing light of our wild existences.

I am inspired by the apostles of the Bible, the ones who personally walked with Christ, and how they spent the remainder of their lives trying to understand a man with whom they shared only three years. The gospel message is not a one-time lesson for beginners—it's a lifetime of exploration.

More than ten years ago, I set to out to discover, for myself, the wonder of who He is. I badgered God with endless "whys":

- Why did You create us?

- Why did You give us a tree that lured us to sin?

- How can You be love and yet show such awful judgment to so many?

- Why does a God of love allow a nation to destroy foreign people groups?

- Why all the junk about animal sacrifices when You knew You would send Your Son?

- ❦ Why not just send Him first and get it over with?
- ❦ Why did you spend 4 thousand years preparing the world for Your Son?
- ❦ Why send Your Son to earth for just three years?

Over the course of ten years, pursuing answers to these and other questions, I have shed many tears—some in anger, some in frustration, some in pain—but most in wonder and joy at discovering who the Father really is and the great lengths He has gone to teach us about His love. My life truly has been forever changed.

God Is Love

I have been mystified by that one thought, warring with it incessantly. It has won. I am dead. I have stripped myself of the garments of my own vainglory and left them on the road as the rags they are. I have presented myself to love, naked and ashamed, begging to be clothed in its garments. Whatever remains of my old life, the old me—I don't want it back. I left most of it somewhere between Chapters 4 and 5.

You, dear reader, are all that I have left and all that I stand to gain—the jewel in my crown and the reason that I have pursued this course. I hope that by knowing the Father and His love, I might find an *overflowing* harvest of kindred souls to share this journey to Heaven. The road is long and hard, but not without its rewards.

To you, I offer my sincerest thanks for taking the time to read my journal. May you find in my thoughts a warm encouragement to pursue the deeper things of God.

In the Father's love,
Joshua M. Jost

CHAPTER ONE

In the Beginning...

*T*he *Artist of Creation* carefully arranges His canvas. He places one planet in an empty universe—no stars, no sun—just one dark planet in one dark, consuming universe.

After carefully mixing His paints He lays down the first color with a gentle, deliberate stroke of the brush.

Light! Red. Blue. Green. Yellow. Orange. Light!

No sun, no stars, no moon, no beginning and no ending—just light, the most basic of all elements on earth. Without light, it would be impossible to enjoy the beauty of creation. The beauty of light is not within itself, but in the object that it illuminates.

The spinning planet glimmers; bright, sparkling waters refract the light, shining, beaming, glowing white!

Then the Creator separates light from darkness.

It seems so normal to live in a world where light and darkness are separate. The Creator could have made them co-exist, but He didn't. Instead, He created light and darkness to exist in a constant state of battle. Darkness cannot exist in the presence of light. Darkness exists only in the absence of light.

Often we speak of opposites as two objects that stand in equal opposition to each other. This is not true of light and darkness. Darkness does not truly oppose light; it just exists in its absence—if we can say that it truly exists. You cannot turn darkness on and you cannot create it. You can only turn light off.

How many other things have we considered opposites that do not stand in equal opposition to each other?

God and satan?
Right and wrong?
Heaven and hell?
Love and hate?

Later chapters play with these ideas, but right now the great Artist is at work again.

He plunges His hands into the ocean-covered planet like a child picking up sand at the beach. Here and there He piles bits of earth, making the planet look like one big jumbled mess. Imagine watching a sculptor at work. All we see is a pile of clay, but the sculptor sees the finished product.

"This bit is going to be China, that part over there will some day be Africa, and right here is a special little piece—it will be called Israel." Continents, peninsulas, islands, mountains, ridges, valleys, beaches, craters appear. Hands shape, mold, and sculpting the earth. Fingers create ridges, His thumbprint leaves a valley. No stone is out of place; every curve and line is carefully thought out and positioned to perfection.

And now, vibrant colors burst forth. The brush flows across brown and gray continents with green, red, blue, purple, yellow, orange, and every color imaginable.

Grass grows on plains, ferns in the jungle, cacti in the desert, trees in the forests and marshlands, and flowers…flowers everywhere! The infinite detail and beauty of every leaf, needle, petal, blade, spore—all are intricately designed.

The Creator makes vegetables: cucumbers, broccoli, potatoes, carrots, peas, corn, and even lima beans. And fruit: apples, oranges, plums, peaches, mangos, guava, and grapes. All of it is pleasant to taste, beautiful to behold.

My translation of the Bible says, *"God saw that it was good."* That may be a bit of an understatement. The Hebrew dictionary[1] says: "Good, pleasant, excellent, lovely, delightful," and my favorite, "beautiful." The Creator made it all breathtaking—made with pleasure to create pleasure! (See Genesis 1:1-31.)

He could have made the world flat, but He didn't. He could have made it black and white, but He didn't. And He didn't have to make flowers.

Why Did He Make Flowers?

Consider a rose. What purpose does it fulfill? You can enjoy its fragrance, gaze at its beauty, but it is meaningless otherwise. Consider a rose in a field of grass; you would think nothing of trampling the grass, yet you wouldn't consider stepping on the rose. Why not?

Why did He make beauty…and what is it anyway? Beauty is simply that in which we find goodness, purpose, and value. Beauty teaches us to appreciate things that are good: a sunset, the softness of a baby's skin, a bird's song, the fragrance of a flower, the taste of a grape, the heart of another.

But, "Beauty is in the eye of the beholder," some say. Maybe they are right. Maybe we are all learning to behold beauty for what it really is. Maybe, as we discover the source of all beauty—the Creator—we learn what true beauty is.

In the Book of Romans, chapter 1, verse 20, God says that through creation, His character has been clearly painted, so that we are without excuse (loosely paraphrased).

The Artist of all artists poured Himself into His creation: no stone misplaced, no color too dull or too radiant. It was all a perfect expression of His heart. He formed a masterpiece and placed His signature upon it, declaring, "This is Me. Study creation and you will see My smile, My mind, My heart, My purpose."

The Father of creation made beauty because He loves to take that which has no life or purpose and make something of value and destiny. Through the process He reveals a part of Himself, a part of His pure, perfect beauty.

For a moment, the Creator turns away from the earth to prepare His next color. He forms a molten ball of fire and causes the earth to revolve around it. Then He creates the moon and causes it to revolve around the earth. Now planets dot our galaxy; all of them held to the sun by an invisible force.

 Now light has an origin.
Now time has a reference.

The sun shines on our planet, feeding the wind, rain, plants, animals, and humanity with warmth and light, giving life to the world.

This one source of life was the first message of the Father to His creation: that everything is dependent upon one source, one perfectly good source, and one source that is not of our world. It is apart from our world, from the heavens, shining eternal goodness upon our lives. Although too bright for us to behold, the sun governs our world by itself and by its reflection on our moon, bringing light into the dark night.

The Creator prepares another color and His brush paints another layer. Beauty and complexity grow.

He touches the brush to the sea and it dances with living creatures: dolphins skimming the surface of the water, schools of fish shimmering with bright colors, sharks lurking behind rocks, and many other creatures hiding at the bottom of the deep blue ocean.

His brush reaches land and birds fly, cheetahs run, and elephants trumpet. The lion roars for the first time and the earth resounds. Yet there is no fear among animals, for there is no food chain. The lion lies down with the lamb. The world is a peaceful, welcoming place.

Now the Creator begins His final creation—His greatest masterpiece. This one is not just another part of the creation; this one resembles the image of the Creator like a son resembles his father. This one will know the Artist not just as Creator, but as Father; and the Father will lead him, not like a servant, but like His child. Their love for each other will be special.

Man Made in the Father's Image

The Creator goes to work, meticulously designing every part of His first son to match every part of Himself. Eyes see light. Ears hear sound. Fingers touch the petals of a flower and appreciate its delicacy; a heart appreciates its beauty.

Creation is made for man to enjoy, learn, and study. Every brush stroke teaches the student about the teacher.

Thinking about how carefully and passionately the Creator etched my fingerprints inspires wonder. You and I were made by Him in His image, each different, original, special!

When the Creator designed the animals, they were unique and new, a complete product of creativity. But when He made man He did something different. He looked to His own being and makeup and patterned man after Himself. Mankind resembles the Creator like a child resembles his father.

When you gaze into the eyes of a child, you see the child's father. When you appreciate a child's beauty, you attribute it to the parent. When you look at mankind, what do you see?

Red, yellow, black, white—they are all precious in His sight. Even the most evil men to walk the planet are all-precious to Him, and are created with a purpose. The Creator loves them all, and they broke His heart.

The Creator tenderly laid His first son in a bed of grass in the midst of a beautiful garden, a special home, and a place to explore the Creator's perfect beauty. Then He looked upon what He had made and said, "It is very beautiful." (See Genesis 1:31.)

The Breath of Life

Blue sky. A gentle breeze. The sound of water trickling in a brook. A bird chirping in the distance. The first man is suddenly ware of his existence. His mind, a clean slate, takes in the first observations of life.

His first thoughts are questions: What is this? Where am I? Who am I? How did I get here? Questions we all think even now. Many questions but no answers. Confusion clouds the mind like darkness. There is no fear, only questions.

"Good morning, My son," he hears. Man, as he was named, meets his Creator. Man finds his source. The dark void of questions disappears in the presence of light. The voice of the Creator dispels darkness.

I have often wondered what that first meeting was like. What was it like to gaze into the eyes of the Creator and see the love in them as He proudly gazed back? In that love, questions were answered. Without words, but with one look, the mind understood: He created me. He loves me. This is my Daddy. Like a newborn baby calmed by a mother's voice, man was at peace in the presence of his Daddy. Father loved son and son had not a worry in the world.

Standing in the garden, gazing deeply into the eyes of the Creator, man saw eternity. He saw a love not affected by the winds of time and the wounds of journeys, not subject to the whims of temporary emotions or blind attractions.

What Is Love?

Love's meaning and essence have puzzled man since the beginning of creation. Think of painters attempting to capture the Eiffel

Tower on canvas, when they haven't been to Paris to see it. Instead, each artist peers at the work of others, trying to imagine what it might look like, and each painting becomes less real and more abstract until at last the paintings become whatever each painter wants it to be. The only way to truly behold the Eiffel Tower is to see it for yourself, not secondhand, but in person, on the streets of Paris.

Similarly, you can only really understand love when you view it from its eternal source, in the eyes of the Father, the Creator and source of love. In His eyes you see a love that looks upon everyone, at all times, and desires to transform each life into a thing of beauty—just like creation.

Love desires life. It seeks to create, grow, and protect life until it flourishes into a thing of goodness and beauty. Through love seeds become flowers, couples become parents, children become adults, ideas become realities. When you truly love someone, you become unconcerned with your own needs as his needs fill your heart; the deeper your love, the greater your concern for the other.

In a world where everyone is consumed with his own needs, there is little room for love. The greater your concern for your own needs, the less room love has in your heart. The Father designed this world to be a place where you need not be concerned with your needs, because He will fulfill all your needs and more.

Love gives purpose, mercy, wisdom, hope, power, time, strength, peace, identity, meaning, shelter, light, for *life*. It is the Father's nature; He is life-creating life through love.

Life is far more than a state of existence; it is ever flourishing, growing, building, improving, learning, and renewing itself over and over again, from beauty to glorious beauty.

✿ *The Beauty of Love* ✿

The Bible says that the Father gave man a command: *"Be fruitful and multiply, fill the earth and tame it"* (see Gen. 1:28). Man was given the keys and told to use them. He was given the throne of the earth. It was his, a giant garden for him to cultivate.

Why?

- ❦ Why did the Father give man an earth that needed to be cultivated?

- ❦ Why not just give him a maintenance-free playground?

- ❦ Was the earth created for man or the Father to enjoy?

- ❦ Was man king of the earth or a gardener taking care of the palace grounds?

- ❦ What could man give to the Father that He didn't already have?

If the Father could create the earth merely by speaking, then certainly He could take care of it the same way.

- ❦ Why did the Father burden man with such a command?

- ❦ Was man to be just a slave?

- ❦ Was he created to keep the Father's science lab project going?

- ❦ What kind of God would create man just to police His creation?

- ❦ Why did the Father go to all the work of specially creating a man from His image just to make him a gardener?

Last week, I held in my hands a masterpiece, an impressionist water painting of remarkable beauty. The artist is an up-and-coming talent of whom I am particularly fond. There may not be much of a market for her work right now, but I think it's worth the price that I have paid for it. It is proudly displayed in the most honored place in our home—the refrigerator door. The artist is my five-year-old daughter, Iona, and the painting is of my wife, "Mummy."

What is so special about this masterpiece?

The picture's value is found in the heart of the artist. A little girl gave this picture every bit of creative talent that she had and proudly presented it to me knowing that I would be amazed and pleased at what she had created. My satisfaction was found in her efforts, and her satisfaction in my gratitude.

How wonderful! A little girl, my daughter, drew a picture just to please me! Many people spend a great deal of money for a painting by an artist they never knew. This young artist was learning to create beauty for my pleasure and for hers.

What can man do for the Father? The same thing a child does for a parent. When we give our lives and abilities to Him, He proudly hangs them on the refrigerator door of Heaven. The world was created as a book full of paper and a box full of crayons for us to draw pictures for the Father.

The Father specially created mankind to be His children. He desired to provide life full of beauty and wonder, so that we in turn would desire to give Him the best of our abilities, to cultivate a world full of life—beautiful, glorious, wonderful life.

The Father created a universe of beauty, by His love. He set man in a garden of beauty to teach and reveal His love. Man was given a world to fill with life, to model His love. Resembling the Father, man was created to bring light out of darkness, order out of chaos, beauty out of blandness, love out of need. You and I were created to be the image of the Father's love on earth.

22

🌀 *Love's Companion* 🌀

Animals of every kind, creature after creature, male and female, father and mother, all of creation was blessed with companionship, except man. Something was missing.

Beginning with subtle emptiness, a pain was growing in man's heart. In the fullness of time it flourished into full-fruited loneliness. He longed for a companion to share his experiences, someone to love and care for, as the Father loved him.

If the animals could birth life out of love in the act of procreation, why couldn't he?

Why had the Father created him without equal; created him alone? This seeming blemish of imperfection was no absent-minded mistake, or technical design fault; this omission was engineered for a purpose. The Father wanted man to know loneliness for a moment, to understand that love fills the vacuum of being alone as light chases away darkness; fire gently heats a cold room; words draw meaning to a blank page; rain cools a hot dry desert.

We were all created with the need for companionship; this void in us begs an answer. No matter how clever, rich, good looking, powerful, or perfect we are, we cannot buy, coerce, manipulate, or engineer love. We can only receive it humbly, when it is offered, and can only give it at the price of our own lives.

There is a deep emptiness in the love-yourself world. It is a godless, dark and cold place, the true opposite of all love. Self creates a vacuum of loneliness so great that it consumes and destroys beauty. Without companionship, the focus too easily falls on self.

Look at those people the world calls most successful and observe how they have sought unto themselves great love, power, and admiration. Many lead lives filled with emptiness. They live on film-set façades within cardboard walls that evaporate in the wind, masquerading great beauty and success with a veneer of "bling" that is only skin deep. Wherever they go, they leave a trail of broken hearts, ruined lives, and bitter tears. They destroy those around them, consuming the lives of others to feed their own voracious and unquenchable appetites. They are not merely alone; they are beggarly, blind, and hopeless.

Instead, I would like to lead you to where true wealth is hidden. Deep into the heart of city ghettos, war-torn countries and famished farmlands; to places where there are those who have given up every outward appearance of wealth to find true riches of love so great that you will stand awe. For their wealth is invested in the lives of others.

Who are they?

They...shed tears for those who have none; bring warm food to frozen hands; touch wounds too deep for scalpels; remember the dead whom the world forgot.

They...polish the worthless into glorious diamonds; adorn the ugly in fine beauty; and anoint the putrid with fragrant perfume.

They...do not possess gold—they *are* gold. Everything they touch becomes beautiful because they have the power to create beauty. They are rich, beyond your wildest dreams!

Love fills the vacuum of loneliness, ugliness and death, with companionship, beauty, and life!

Love's Gift

Man's eyes opened for the second time. What was she? Focusing on his new beloved for the first time, he beheld beauty. An attraction, an invisible force was drawing him to her. It was love alive, warmly aglow.

Driven by the loneliness in his heart, he had come to the Father, heart in hand, to ask for a companion to love. He could have asked, selfishly, for greater love for himself, but for what point in a world where he was already perfectly loved?

Longing sought fulfillment.
Love sought life.

Like his Father, the son was learning to shine love into the darkness of loneliness. In a sense, his love had given her life; buried beneath her bosom, embracing her heart was one of his ribs, removed from his own body. The foundation of life in her was him. She was woman, taken out of man.

Woman would find pleasure in giving life to her children; man would find pleasure in the life that he gave to her; and the Father would find pleasure in the life that He gave them.

As their gaze met, satisfaction filled his heart.
He discovering her, for whom life did impart.
One in flesh and blood, now naked unashamed.
She discovering him, for whom she had been made.
Loneliness had vanished, love to him had come.
Forever to dote upon her as two become one.

Their blood, the very life that flowed within them, was now married in a spiritual act of unity as they were intertwined together and shared a special bond called covenant. No longer two separate beings, they were now one flesh, sharing the same purpose, mind, and thought. Life flowing from one to the other. Love flowing between them.

But something went terribly wrong....

Endnote

1. ARS8 Lexicon to the Old and New Testaments from the Hebrew-Greek Key Study Bible New American Standard Edition, Edited by Spiros Zodhiates, TH.D., published by AMG publishers.

CHAPTER TWO

Forbidden Fruit

*H*earts pounding, feet trembling, they quietly approach step by cautious step. Never had they been so close to danger.

Water trickled over pebbles, stones, rocks. A river ran through hills, valleys, and ravines. Cool, fresh, and clean, the stream fed life into the garden, its waters the life flow of the earth as blood is the life flow of the body. And upon its gentle wake flowed the nutrients so desperately needed to grow, live, and survive. Its moisture soaked into the soil and fed into the roots of a tree, a tree of mystery.

Why was this tree here in the garden of love?

If the garden was made in perfect love and everything in it was perfectly beautiful and good, then the tree must in itself be perfectly beautiful and good; yet, its fruit held the poison of death.

A strange irony. How can it be? Death and beauty hanging from one tree?

Across the garden grew another tree, the tree of life, its fruit endowed with pure nourishment from Heaven. Two trees in exact opposition. Why? To man and woman, these two trees represented, in simplest form, the choice of life and death.

I Wonder...

Curiosity can be your best friend or worst enemy, leading you to great discoveries or evil snares. It begins with "I wonder…" and can end practically anywhere in the world. All the greatest inventions, monuments, battles, books and songs began with "I wonder…"

The Father gave man and woman the ability to wonder, to dream about what can be—to live beyond what is. It is the nature we share with the Father, to create, discover, and explore. It is not limited to what is, but pursues what is not and brings it to life.

The wonders are our choice. They are the gaze of our hearts, imagining what we can create, do, or give life to. We choose our gaze. We choose what we long after and therefore what we pursue.

But why did He give them a choice? Because love is a choice. Man and woman were created by choice; they were the fruit of God's "I wonder…" There was no obligation in God to create man and woman, to give them life; it was His pure creative desire at work.

And just as simply, man and woman were given the choice to wonder, to pursue the path of life or the path of death. The ultimate act of love by parents is to give their children the choice to reject life or pursue it. It may be painful sometimes, even heartbreaking, for a parent to watch a child struggle; yet unless there is a choice, the child will never value the decision to live.

In the darkness of the love-yourself world, wonders are filled with the emptiness of living in the lonely vacuum of self. They are hopeless and destructive with no gain and no lasting reward.

I wonder if I can…get away with it? Still be friends? Pay them later? Sell this lie? Have this fling?

I wonder if hell exists?

But those seeking the true riches of love, the beauty and life that comes from the Father, ask different questions. Their wonderings search for beauty in others, for hope in despair, and life in death.

I wonder if…frowns can smile? Tears can dance? Sorrows can sing? Ugly can turn beautiful? Bad can be good? Selfishness can be love?

I wonder if Heaven exists?

But why heaven and hell? They are God's answers to the ultimate "I wonders."

Heaven is the ultimate answer to what love can give: the perfect life filled with beauty, peace, happiness and goodness, paradise for an eternity, unending, without measure.

It is the place where the Father is, beautiful because He is there. You appreciate Heaven because you appreciate the Father. Everything is a mirror of His character. It is like an architect who has created his house with every bit of creative expression that he has. The house is a reflection of his hands, and his hands are a reflection of his heart, without limitations.

I believe that the Father made it a place that you dream about so that when you arrive, your heart has never felt so at home.

It is sad to consider those who do not desire Heaven. Those who decide to shut out the love of the Father and let evil fill it, those who decide that the love of God will not bring satisfaction, those who seek their own needs and pleasure.

I wonder if we choose discontentment. I wonder if discontentment is not really based on our needs, but rather on the direct result of looking within. I wonder if discontentment is really about saying to God, You haven't been good to me. I wonder if the first step to shunning love is refusing to give love because we are wondering if we have been loved enough.

Hell is the Father's ultimate answer to the "I wonders" of evil and the pursuit of self: loneliness, pain, hatred, hurt, misery and hopelessness, death—unending, forever.

What is hell? Well if Heaven is the place where God is, hell is the place where God isn't. It is the place in the furthest reaches of God's conscience creation, where He is not. Hell is the place where God has removed everything that is of Him, including life, goodness, happiness, pleasure, and purpose. Everything but basic consciousness is gone, leaving nothing but darkness and evil—and with them despair, pain, hopelessness. It is the vacuum of life.

When you reject the Father, you also reject life and goodness, because they cannot exist apart from God. Hell is what most are pursuing. They may not say as much, but when their lives are bent on the rejection of the love and goodness of the Father, their actions declare the answer.

Hell is not satan's domain; it is the place waiting for all those who reject life and love to pursue self and death. It is justice, created to persuade satan and anyone else who would pursue this course to turn away. It is not an empty threat or a veiled reality; it is more truthful and more fearful than anything that can be imagined.

The Fearful Protection of the Father

We weren't meant to discern good and evil by personal knowledge; we have chosen to do so. The Father's solution is fear. It is love guiding us away from death. In love He said to man and woman, "Do not eat of the fruit, it will kill you." (See Genesis 2:17.)

Early in life a child learns to distinguish bad from good: bitter tastes from sweet tastes, scary sights and sounds from pleasant ones, pain from pleasure. A loving father teaches a child to fear him because in his arms, the child learns that the father's voice will protect him from harm. The only fear the child needs is the loving discipline of parents. A child, who does not fear, faces a world of fears, ranging from hot fires, bad tastes, scary sights, and loud noises to many more harmful fears throughout life. He comes to fear everything because he learns by experience what is harmful or good for him, rather than learning from a loving parent.

Thus fear stands in the place of judgment to teach us to trust in love. Fear itself is the beginning of trust. It is the recognition of the true source of danger.

God is the ultimate danger.

We fear everything, because we are in control of our own lives. When we recognize, however, that the One who holds the universe and life and death and Heaven and hell in His hands is the only thing we need to fear; that not a sparrow falls to the ground without the Father's knowledge; when we come to invest every fear that we have in Him, then we are free from all other fears.

The Father holds the entire universe in His hands. There is nothing He can't protect us from, when we fear Him.

Heaven and hell exist because love exists. It is our decision to pursue the course of love, to seek the perfect beautiful life of Heaven over the horrific ugly death of hell. It is up to us to choose, every day: to love or not to love.

In the Father's perfect justice, He gives to us what we truly desire—life or death, Heaven or hell.

"Has God said that you may not eat from any tree in this garden?" spoke the serpent hanging loosely about one of the branches. Man and woman were suddenly aware of the strange presence of evil. Death's advocate, satan himself, looked into their eyes, his forked tongue hissing deception. (See Genesis 3:1.)

He had come to kill. He had come to steal. He had come to destroy with deception as his ploy. His question, though appearing innocuous, planted a deadly seed. Man and woman began to wonder—wonder about their limitations, wonder what they were missing, wondering within.

"God has said that we can eat from all the trees, but we can't eat or touch this tree or we will die," the woman answered. Already, the seed at work, she had added to God's commandment. He had only commanded that they not eat of the tree, yet her mind was changing. The Father who loved her was now becoming to her a tyrant with rules. (See Genesis 3:2-3.)

The seed of doubt was planted in her mind.

For the first time, she was questioning the love and goodness of their Father, whom she knew, and inhaling the lies of this serpent, whom she knew not.

"You will not die!" he hissed, *"God knows that if you eat from this tree, you will become like Him, knowing good from evil."* The words arose from his tongue like smoke ascending into the air, filling their lungs with the black deception of knowledge. (See Genesis 3:4-5.)

The very thought was intoxicating.

The serpent laid before them the ultimate temptation of sin: the pursuit of knowledge for power. It was a mesmerizing lure, like a jewel just out of reach, offering them the ability to rule their own destinies by controlling life and death.

How many businessmen, scientists, philosophers, pastors, and teachers have built their lives upon this deception to acquire the power to control their own destiny? Whether they feel that they are using it for good is beside the point. Dictators, politicians, and religious leaders have imposed great suffering upon multitudes of people under the spell of this knowledge, because they believe their brand of good to be good for all.

We were never meant to hold this power. Ours was simply to trust and obey, living in innocent love. When we see this love in children we recognize it as beautiful, knowing inwardly that it is a good thing to see a child trusting her parents. When we are older we expect that a little worldly knowledge will do us some good, and we feast ourselves upon its fruit. Just in case we seem foolish for doing so, we label those who prefer the innocence of trust and love as "simple" and "naïve."

Doubt had entered man and woman's hearts; their introspection had given birth to discontentment. The temptation was hanging before them and they were growing hungry for it. Should they live as naïve slaves before a tyrant master who really didn't care for them? Or, should they grab the fruit and become masters themselves?

But, how could they doubt the goodness of God? An entire world was at their disposal, with only one tree out of their reach; yet they doubted. They were loved, protected, cherished, prized even; yet they doubted.

With the Father they walked, spoke, played, grew, in the garden of His protection; yet they doubted. They knew His voice, yet they doubted. Discontentment was their choice.

The woman took hold of the fruit, broke it from the tree, consciously and purposely bit into it, and gave to her husband who did the same. For the first time, they had rejected the goodness of God. For the first time, they stepped into the darkness of evil. For the first time, they knew good from evil.

Sweet sin upon their lips
Pleasure their mouths found
Bitter poison chilled their bones
In death's grasp they now were bound.

A spiritual shockwave roared through the earth as its king and queen had opened the door of sin. The river of love that flowed from Heaven through them to the earth was stemmed; the power of death was loosed like a fearsome beast.

If life is a state of regeneration—living beings continually renewing, and growing; things becoming more and more beautiful, healthy and alive—then death is a state of degeneration: things failing, falling apart, devolving into ugliness and destruction. This became the state of our world, like a clock winding down.

Life and death are not an end, but a direction, a road, that continues for eternity.

The serpent slid quietly but triumphantly into the bushes.

Man and woman beheld their world with new eyes, eyes filled with fear. They were no longer in the safe boundaries of love, but had stepped into an entire world of fear. They were naked, ashamed, vulnerable, and exposed, their curse driving them from the very One who had given them life.

The Father entered the garden in great sadness that day, already knowing His son and daughter had rejected Him. But He did not reject them; instead He called out to them, hoping that in spite of their newfound fear, they would trust Him.

Man and woman heard His voice and knew they couldn't hide from Him any longer. Instead, hoping the Father would overlook their sin, they hid their shame with fig leaves and blame, just as man today covers his shame with wealth, knowledge, power, and religion. All of these ploys are foolish in the eyes of the Creator.

The Father burned with anger, not the anger that brings hatred, but the anger that brings tears—anger directed, not toward them, but toward what separated them from Him.

Their sin had created such fear and separation from the Father that there was no way they could ever share the intimacy and trust that they had known before.

> The Father was perfect;
> they were imperfect.
> The Father was light;
> they were darkness.

> The Father was good;
> they were evil.

I cannot judge man and woman for what they did, because I have done it too. If I judge them, I judge myself as well. I have sinned and fallen short of the Father's love. I have stepped up to that tree with doubt in my heart and enjoyed the fruit of sin. What's worse is that I have felt the bitter pain of its poison, yet I have gone back for more.

I wish I could claim innocence, but it is not mine to claim. I wish I could bury the past, but it lives on in my mind. The chasm that separates the Father from man is our choice. We have chosen it and we like it.

This, dear reader, is sin: we doubt the love of the Father and we seek our own desires. Sin is that moment when we step outside of His perfect purpose for us and we step into our purposes for ourselves. It is far more than breaking a rule or making a mistake; it is the entire course of life, the tree of sin, the road to death.

Some, like Eve the woman, do so because they are deceived; this is called a shortfall. Others, like Adam the man, do so knowing full well the path that they are pursuing; this is called rebellion. But still others, like the serpent, go beyond rebellion, bending the truth into deception, infecting others with it, spreading it like an ugly disease; this is called warping. And for obvious reasons, the Father most actively opposes those who spread warping, because of its devastating effects upon others.

Some wonder if the Father was at fault because He knew they would fall. It seems like a rational argument, but it is not. As a father myself, I know that my children will make mistakes because they are gifted with free will. Because I love them, I plan for their

38

mistakes, but I don't purpose them. I plead with them not to make unwise decisions, and I do all that is in my power to prevent their fall. In the end, I have to give them the freedom to make their own choices; otherwise, they will never understand love. It is important to realize, though, that it is not through sinning that we know love; it is through fear.

Ultimately, we choose our wonders, we choose our doubts, we choose our discontentments, and we choose our sin.

Thankfully the chapter closes with a promise—a promise from the Father that through woman's childbearing, One would come to crush the serpent, the father of sin. Life would come through her womb and take victory over death. In the darkest moments in history, the Father sends forth the glimmer of life.

Woman became Eve, the *mother of all living,* a reminder of the promise.

CHAPTER THREE

The Father

*M*an wasn't created to walk the path of life alone. He wasn't created to grow up in a world ruled by nature's "survival of the fittest" law.

We were created to love.

We were created to live under the care, shelter and protection of a Father and to give the same life to others. We were created to grow under the gentle wing of someone greater. Those who have gone without this love have gone hurting and empty, thinking that life is about fending for your self, thinking that a father's love is unimportant, thinking that those who trust in fathers lean upon a rickety old crutch.

Children became parents, having children becoming parents, having children becoming parents, having children not knowing the Father. The children He had fathered rejected Him and ran toward the tree of self-indulgence, leaving behind the ways of love and entering the ways of darkness. The true Father became the rejected Father.

At the center of the pursuit of self is the vacuum of sin—a black hole within that slowly sucks out life day by day. It has a voracious hunger that can only be quenched by the power of life itself: love.

Here is the dilemma: when everyone pursues self, no one pursues love; and the world unravels, becoming chaotic, confused, and wild. Man knows that he cannot live without love, so he lives in a state of quid-pro-quo, tit-for-tat, I'll-scratch-your-back-if-you-scratch-mine, kind of pseudo love. We need the unity and peace that comes from loving each other, yet we don't want to completely pursue love. So we pursue only enough to get what we need. This is an existence on the fringe of life. Taking as much life as we can get, while giving as little as possible, results in misery.

Thus society depends upon a moral code to create enough love to maintain some balance of justice while giving enough "freedom" for the pursuit of self.

These moral codes must be empowered by a philosophy, to give weight and authority to them. Thus man creates gods to justify his actions and pursuits. Since the beginning of time, he has dressed up his philosophies and moral codes with a god of some type, who is normally no more than man dressed in superior powers but bearing the same emotions and weaknesses. The gods are merely a reflection of their makers, as any creation reflects its creator. They are simply humanity glorified.

It's easy to think of the ancients as simpletons. Our philosophies of evolution have taught us that they were less developed than we. The truth, however, is far different. Scientists today still marvel at the knowledge possessed by the ancients. They understood the nature of the world and the stars; and knew how to harness powers or "energies" for their own purposes.

No, these men were not merely "born yesterday"; they were possessors of great power, the wisest of their day, filled with that forbidden fruit—knowledge and its companion, pride. For the purpose of knowledge is pride. By it, men lift themselves up and make themselves great. Pride at its core is the pursuit of I—I can, I will, I did—standing in direct opposition to love.

False Religion Born

Although small, a mere colony really, it was the epicenter of the world. The entire tribe of humans was gathered in one place, on an open plain along the banks of the river that had once flowed from the Garden. Something spectacular was rising from among them, a monument of epic proportions, a tower called the "Gate of God".

Stone upon stone, layer upon layer, deception upon deception, the human tribe erected a towering monstrosity, a pathway to divine love. Yet behind the noble dressing of religion was nothing more than man's knowledge and man's pride, dressed up as God's. Man was trying to reach up to God; trying to lift himself up, raise himself up through his knowledge. It was the same forbidden fruit of knowledge, being tasted over and over again.

The Father, watching from Heaven, was grievously angered by their deception. The world had turned their backs to Him; they had rejected His life and love; and now they were doing it in the name of God! He blew upon their creation from the heavens, destroyed their monument, and confused their language—demonstrating to them what is the end result of their efforts, the deception of their wonders: confusion. (See Genesis 11:4-9.)

The fruit of our deception is confusion. The world may try to sell its deception under many other brand names—understanding, peace, and unity—but ultimately its true colors will show. The sheepskin will slip and the wolf will have its day.

Babel, the *Gate of God,* took on new meaning from that day. The world will forever remember it for its babbling confusion. Or will it?

And so it began....

Clothes, utensils, tools, mementos, food, and water. Each packed bag was a symbol of hope: hope of a new home, a new land, new friends, new experiences, and new life. It was the beginning of a journey. The journey began in a prosperous city called Ur not far from where the infamous tower once stood...and fell.

Abram was about to leave behind everything that he knew. It would all be dead to him. There were few reasons to qualify Abram for the task set before him. Very few. Only one really: he knew how to listen.

The Father had planted a seed in Abram's heart, a small seed. The seed would become a tree. The tree would bring forth fruit. The fruit would bring healing for the fruit of sin. And the nations of the earth would come to find it. It was a tree that would bridge the gap between Creator and creation, sinful and perfect, man and God. But for now, it was nothing more than a seed, a tiny little promise to a man who had nothing more to give than a listening ear.

Why does God choose to speak to some so clearly, yet others never hear His voice?

Why is it that God chose to speak to Abram? He was a simple man, definitely not a superhero worthy of fathering of a nation. As a matter of fact, he was a bit of a coward. He would tell two kings that his wife was his sister. In each case he feared that the king would kill Abram and claim his wife. Instead, Abram just gave her away.

But God did speak to Abram and promised to make him a great nation, through which all other nations of the earth would be blessed. Why? Because Abram listened.

Abram didn't need to build a tower to hear God. He only needed to listen and believe. The truth is that God speaks. He speaks so loudly that the earth rumbles with His voice, the mountains shake, and the waves roll. He has written His words across the sky, the ground, and the sea, yet we cannot see or hear them. Why not?

Many hear, but few listen.

The mind is slave to the heart. It will explain and rationalize that upon which the heart sets its gaze. If the heart has chosen to be its own master, the mind will prove that there is no other. Even though the Father may call so loudly that the ground shakes, the mind will merely acknowledge an earthquake. Our heart determines the reality that we see.

In a world of rejection and unbelief, Abram believed. When all others would have dismissed God's words as lies or deception, Abram believed. When all others would have joined company with the warped serpent, Abram believed.

To believe in someone's words, you must believe in who he is, for his words are only as good as his character. When you believe that God is love, you must believe that His words will come true, because to do otherwise would be contrary to love.

God speaks promises to us, his children, yet we won't believe. Look through His Word, there is promise upon promise of God's faithfulness to love and care for us. These promises are meaningless if we do not believe in the promise giver. If we do not believe His words, we reject His character. If we reject His character, we reject Him.

His voice is everywhere:
Look at the beauty of the sunset.
"I"
Hear the pounding waves of the ocean.
"Love"
See the baby in your arms.
"You."

Did you hear it? The Father can use the cry of a baby, the beauty of creation, the tragedy of death, or the very thoughts in your head to speak to you. You will never hear Him until you are ready to believe, ready to believe in the most important thought that He has for you: "I love you." His love is the pledge of His desire to give you life—eternal, unlimited, and beautiful.

The love of the Father meets you where you are, in a bread line, hospital bed, or prison. He says, if you follow Me, trusting in My love for you, I will lead you from this place of death to life. You may be surrounded by utter misery and failure; it doesn't matter. This promise is a tiny seed called hope. When you believe in the promise, hope takes root in your heart. When you pack your bags and leave your old world behind, you open the door for the light of love to shine upon you and for hope to sprout into faith.

True love has one great condition: that you follow. It requires faith to follow from the bread line, hospital, or prison to its home where you can be safe, healed, and free.

Abram listened and believed, and the Father counted it to him as righteousness. God was willing to overlook his sin purely because Abram was willing to listen and believe. Faith is nothing more than trusting in someone to fulfill his promises. It may be a parent promising to always look after a child, a husband promising to care for his wife, or two friends promising to look after each other. Trust is the act of believing that love will hold to its promise.

Abram could have sat at home, debating whether or not he actually heard the Father, wondering if he might hear Him again, wondering if he could even trust Him. But he didn't. Instead he set his wonders on the land that was promised and left home.

This was for Abram the beginning of life. In the simple act of faith in love, he was departing the life of sin to learn to walk in the life of love. The Father considered him worthy of life because he had chosen life as his destination and was willing to let the Father lead him there. We can't get there ourselves; we can only do it by the empowering love of the Father.

Abram was no Genghis Khan, Alexander the Great, or even Winston Churchill. The Father chose to start His nation with a simple man following a simple faith. A man whose name means *father*.

The Father could have used the sword
of a conqueror, but He didn't.
He could have used the scepter of
a great leader, but He didn't.
He could have used the mind of
a wise ruler, but He didn't.
His tiny seed was none of these.
Instead he used the heart of a father,
the heart of a barren father.

The Father of creation reflecting
Himself in the father of a nation.

The greater your dreams, the heavier the price.

It was morning, and the sun was setting on the life of this weather-worn Bedouin traveler. His tired, sandaled feet carefully negotiated the rocky slope leading him to the final challenge of his faith. Not long after his trek he would sleep—an eternal sleep with a new-day dawn of joy unlike any he had ever known.

Cresting the mountain he gazed as far as his weary eyes would allow, seeing more in his memories than of the world in front of him. These feet had traveled far and wide, step of faith following step of faith, exploring, with the Father, this wonderful hope—a promised land, a place to build a family and grow a nation. This stretch of terra firma was his dream house, and he had walked its borders imagining what it would look like: fathers and mothers in love, babies born, sons playing, daughters dancing, a nation at peace.

And in the middle of it all, he imagined a great city, a flourishing metropolis, where they would gather to celebrate the love and life given to them and think of their father, who had given his life, leaving everything behind, so that they could live.

He could have settled in the land, living a comfortable but selfish life, feasting on the fruit of his own possessions. But his wonders were set firmly on the hope of fathering a nation, and it was all a living dream, waking him every day from the heavy sleep of reality. He had walked it, touched it, and slept in it. It had created a hunger that he could not fill.

When love calls, it asks you to follow and then leads you on a journey to its home, saying, I will give my life to you, for your life. All that I have is yours: my protection, my provision, my wealth, my wisdom, my understanding, and my strength. All this I will offer you if you will learn to trust and follow me. To do this, you have to leave behind your own possessions to have mine. You must leave your house and your path to come and dwell in my house and walk my path. You cannot have both. You cannot have your life and love's life. It is one life, one body, and one heart.

Furthermore, love says, I am so serious about this commitment that if I ever fail to provide the life I have promised to you, I will curse myself with the death that I am sworn to protect you from experiencing. My life for yours, my death for yours.

This commitment, called *covenant*, was the act of two parties becoming one, sharing their lives; the strong protecting and caring for the weak, the weak devotedly trusting the strong. Out of their relationship, out of their intimacy, life could come forth. It was the same relationship that the Father had intended for man and woman at the beginning.

Just as the Father had built a garden for man and woman to dwell in peace and safety, love creates a house of safety in which life can flourish and grow. Love becomes your husband, literally your *house-band,* banding itself around you.

The Father brought Abram to the Promised Land and showed him all that He would provide for him. He promised to be Abram's shield of protection, offering this same covenant commitment—to build a house for him in this land. In answer, Abram brought a few small animals as a token of his possessions and offered them as a sacrifice to the Father, creating through them a pathway of life for the Father to come and meet him. Thus love teaches us to offer ourselves to Him, giving up our own lives so that we can be filled with love's life. In this place, our lives mingle and become one.

To the ancients, this practice of covenant meant to cut, because in their ritual they always cut and mingled blood to show that two lives had now become one.

As the sun was still high in the sky the sojourner had to ward off the vultures that wished to prey upon him. We also are vulnerable. We have to protect our own possessions until the day our struggles end and the Father causes us to rest in Him. As daylight closed, darkness and sleep fell upon Abram. The Father stepped into the darkness as a bright light. He walked through the pathway of life to form a partnership with Abram, promising to protect Abram and to give him the promised possession—the land.

Abram's possessions—temporary and miniscule in comparison to the Father of Creation—were now the Father's. The Father's possessions—permanent and eternal—would forever be Abram's.

If hope were our destination, and faith the feet that carry us there, covenant is our path, laid straight before us. It is the promise that if we follow it, it will take us surely to our destination. If we wander from it, we know that we have taken our lives again into our own hands.

And Abram Did Wander

He watched the sands slipping through the hourglass of life; watched as time passed, grain after grain of sand. At first he saw the sand gathering as a hill, then a mountain, at the bottom of the glass. Time was running out. Abram's entire promise now hinged on one solitary event: the birth of a son.

The Father waited. Not forgetting, but waiting. Waiting for time, the right time, the time when Abram would know that his child was not just biological reproduction, but a gift from the Father Himself. He was waiting until Abram was at the point of true dependence upon the Father to fulfill his dreams.

It's easy to believe when things are going your way. It's easy to believe when you can clearly see the Father's goodness. But if you only believe in the sun when it's sunny, do you really believe in the sun at all? When the clouds of darkness come, will you hope for sunshine?

Many are fair-weather believers who turn from God as soon as the clouds begin to roll. If you are to know God's goodness, you must believe in Him heart and soul, during good times and bad. Not until He has taken you through the valley of the shadow of death, can He lead you to the majestic peaks. If you follow only when He's going your way, you may not be following at all.

When your wife goes through menopause and your one hope in life is becoming a father, what do you do? Whom do you trust? Do you trust the voice of the great Father? Could you wait? Could you watch the sands of time slip away? The Father had promised, hadn't He? What if He really meant something else? What if there's something that I should have done to make it happen?

It was a good idea really, a simple suggestion, actually customary at the time. *Perhaps my wife is right,* thought Abram. Her servant would make an excellent surrogate mother. All he had to do was get her pregnant and presto, all of the Father's problems would be solved. Abram would have a son to fulfill the Father's promise.

Abram had been born for this; it was his name. From the time he was a baby he heard his parents calling him: Abram! *Father!* Bred into him was this desire to hold a child and to be called *Papa.*

Beyond his breeding, his world considered fatherhood the crowning achievement of life. What point was there to an existence that left no legacy, an existence that left nothing to endure beyond a single lifetime?

In our fast-food, live-for-the-moment, rising-stars culture, we can't quite understand the depth of desire that filled Abram's heart—the desire to build a family that would be spoken of for generations to come. The close-knit families of previous generations are all but extinct.

There was an ache within Abram, a longing desire to love, a vacuum of loneliness. Who can blame this wanna-be dad for his grief! The Father knew the feeling. He had desired people on this earth to love and the world had rejected Him. This nation was to be not just for Abram's joy, but for the Father's as well.

Hoping for a son is difficult enough when youth is your companion. What about when you are old, your wife is beyond childbearing age and all you have to hold on to is a promise from God? Still no problem! If God could create the world and be the source of all love and goodness, it would be easy for Him to cause a woman to reenter menstruation and have a baby.

This was Abram's challenge: trusting in the strength of the Father above rather than his own weak and impotent frame. The Father was waiting for that perfect time in Abram's life, when Abram would know that this son was the son of promise and no other. There was more than the birth of a son at stake. Like can only breed like; for Abram, a father, to become the father of a nation of faithful followers, he would have to learn what it meant to follow faithfully himself. If he was going to give birth to those who would trust in the Father's love, he would have to learn to trust in it fully himself.

When our eyes are fixed on the Father, it is easy to believe. Just take a moment to contemplate who God is. When you gaze into His eyes, you see the love in them. When you look at His hands, you see His awesome power and know that nothing can stop Him from fulfilling His promises.

But when our eyes wander and our heart wonders, the doubts come flooding in. Why has He waited so long? Has He forgotten? Has He lost interest?

Our faith decays.

If the journey of love is faith along the path of commitment toward hope, then the journey into darkness is the exact opposite: doubt along the path of rejection toward the destination of despair and death.

For Abram, a moment of pleasure gave birth to a lifetime of regrets with a son who could never measure up to the purposes that his father desired for him. Ishmael was not the fruit of love but of selfish desire. He would become a nation, but one with a central flaw in its character: the weak enslaved to the desires of the strong—the opposite of love. A nation of people without trust unwilling to believe, unfaithful. Like unfortunately begets like. Yet are we not all infidels, *unfaithful ones,* until we learn to trust in the love of the Father?

If the Father were not so full of love this might have been the end of a very sad story. But His promises are stronger than our sins. The Father met Abram again to renew His commitment. But this time, it would be much deeper. This time, they would share more than possessions. This time, they would share their very lives. The Father asked Abram to covenant with the symbol of his life-giving power, this time, Abram shed his own blood in a rite of circumcision. He was saying to the Father, I give you not just my possessions, but my very life. I will trust you to bring life from me. He was promising total fidelity to the Father.

For Abram's response, the Father changed his name, adding the word *great*. Abram became Abraham the great father, and Sarai became Sarah the great princess.

Abraham had taken upon himself the greatest name in the world. His identity was now invested in the Father's and the Father's in him. Every child born of Abraham would be born not only of Abram, but also of the Father.

It's not enough to be surrounded by Father's love, and the things of His love. We may start in this way, but love takes us deeper. Love its identity including all of its strength and character, and takes upon itself our weakness and need.

Sarah became pregnant and bore a son. His name was Isaac, meaning *laughter*. He was the joy that Abraham had sought after.

And then....

Standing over his only true earthly possession, knife in hand, Abraham was ready to offer up to the Father his last living hope, at the pinnacle of this mountain in the middle of the land of promise. The son of promise was about to become a covenant sacrifice. Though the Father dwelt in Abraham's possessions, and in Abraham himself, the son was all that remained uncommitted.

Abraham looked into eyes that he had loved since birth. He had taught the one behind those eyes to trust completely in him. The son, carefully watching his father, had learned to walk, talk, play, work, love, and live. And now Isaac was trusting fully; preparing even to face death for his father. In this same way, the eyes of Abraham's heart were looking now with complete trust to the Father, believing that He was bigger than death.

How could the Father, the source of all love, ask for Isaac's life? Where was the love in his murder? I imagine that Abraham might have offered a painful smile and told you simply, "Isaac is the Father's promise, and I have no place to argue with how He fulfills His promises."

But in Abraham's determination to destroy his last earthly hope in a promise, all his hope now rested in the Father alone. The Father was pleased. It was only then that the Father stepped in and Abraham was finally free. Free from his self-dependency, free from his mission on earth. Free to rest in the Father's promise.

The Father fulfills His promises in His way and in His time. You can have the confidence that He will fulfill them, but you cannot question how. He is the source of all love and life.

Abraham needed to know that the Father could bring life from death. His son of promise was living proof. Isaac trusted his father to death. Abraham trusted that the Father could bring life from death. Isn't that what we all need to believe?

The Father gave Abraham a ram to replace the offering of his son there on Mount Moriah, the mountain of the Lord's provision. The Father had provided everything that was needed to begin His nation. All that Abraham offered was faith. And with a faithful father and a faithful son, the nation was born. The Father in Heaven *fathered* a nation. He did not conquer a nation, build a nation, or win a nation. His heart always was and always will be a *father's* heart.

CHAPTER FOUR

Pulled From the Water

*T*he Father had blessed her with a son. He was beautiful, a special gift, and she could barely take her eyes off him, even for a moment.

His hands reached for her, his eyes gazed into hers, his smile mimicked hers, and he was completely helpless in her arms. Though he knew her not, yet she loved him and would give her life for him.

She was comforted by the sight of him, yet nervous. His life was cursed. What should she do? The king of their land had issued a decree: any boy born of a Hebrew household must die. How could she subject her son to it? She couldn't do it. No, she couldn't.

What dread filled her soul! What pain tore her heart! Yet looking into his eyes, she was calm again. He was a gift.

Many wondered why God, their God, the God of Abraham their forefather, would allow them to live in such torture. Egypt had been a wonderful place to start with, a haven in a famine where they had grown and prospered. Yet now they were hated. Hated because they had prospered so well. They were driven into slavery and treated like dogs.

Oh Abraham, Abraham, Abraham. Where are the promises of your covenant?

Do you wonder why it seems like God moves so slowly? Why He spends years waiting for the right moment to heal or restore? Why, God, do You wait? How many times have I grown impatient at His patience? How many times have I cried out in anger for Him to respond to my need? I'm forever trying Him, taunting Him, begging Him: God, if You really loved me…

But wait…Do *I* really love *Him?* I may answer "yes," but I know that sometimes it would be dishonest. Am I standing at the cliff edge of my trust, looking into the vast expanse of what is beyond, mad at Him for something that is my own fault?

If faith begins with a decision to follow, unbelief begins with a decision not to follow. When love beckons us to life and we refuse, we declare love to be a lie and we harden our hearts.

Belief and Unbelief

In that vast chasm beyond my comfort zone, I must determine whether or not I will trust His love beyond what I can see. Truth be told, my love has its limits, and beyond them reside the scariest places I know—the places where I am tempted to harden my heart, eat in bitterness, store up anger, and drown in a dark world of "whys."

The woman stood at that chasm. With no end in sight, she had two choices: to let go and give in to her doubts or to trust in the power of her Creator's love.

I have no doubt that many around her gave up. They watched with heartbroken, tear-filled eyes as their sons were ripped mercilessly from their arms and flung into the river, never to be seen again. Inside their hearts welled up with anger and the desire to lash out at the God who would let their babies die. I can't say that I wouldn't have been in that group.

I imagine the gentle waves rolling away from the tiny basket as it was placed into the water, its weight transferred from the loving arms of a sorrowful mother into the buoyancy of a cold and emotionless river.

Tears falling.

Drip. Drip.

"I must believe."

Drip. Drip.

"His love is stronger than death."

Drip. Drip.

Her tears splashed onto the baby's face and then rolled onto his blanket. Again she stared into his beautiful eyes until her courage began to waiver. The baby looked back at her with the trust that melts every parent's heart, the true innocence of every child who believes without question that his or her parent loves fully. That sort of trust even melts the heart of your heavenly Father.

The mother turned away from her boy to gather the courage to do what she must. Many more teardrops followed.

With every bit of resolve left in her, she walked away from her baby, leaving him among the reeds in the river Nile.

Drip, drip.

Her oldest child, her daughter, stayed behind, having been briefed on what to do.

She knew that she was powerless to save her son. Only time was on her side, and only briefly. Yet she knew in her heart—she could feel it within her—the calming voice of her own Father. She felt the power of the story of Abraham in her bones. She knew God's promises. She knew His great power. Though everyone around her doubted, she would believe. She must believe. Though she suffered ridicule, she would believe.

She gave her son away, letting him drift into the arms of her heavenly Father, believing that He loved her son more than she could. He was a living sacrifice.

"Why would God abandon us?" her friends might say. "Is it to make us suffer and struggle? Does He revel in our pain?"

But love begs you to refuse such ideas. Would love wish us to suffer in pain without hope? The truth is that love would gladly rescue us if it were not for our lack of faith. We may ask and cry out for salvation, but do our hearts really agree? Do we really want to leave behind all that we know in this land of death to take up the course of life? If the Father came and asked us to follow, would we be prepared to do so? Would we follow all the way to the Promised Land or would we abandon our pursuit and run back to bondage, worse off than before?

Love will not rescue us until we are ready to follow its path. The Father, a true father, knows when His children are ready to stand the challenge. He will not lead them into a place that would only end in complete failure and disappointment. Some may abandon their own children with such an "I told you so," but not the Father.

Perhaps she could feel His own tears falling on her, flooding her soul, drowning her in the kind of comfort that words shy away from. She was sad, but without the pain of bitterness; sadness mingled in her heart with gratitude for hope.

But her sorrow was soon broken by the sound of her daughter's footsteps running into the house. In the split-seconds that seemed like eternity, her daughter tried to convey a comfort beyond words—salvation, miraculous salvation—and she felt a rush of emotion. The Father had rescued her son, and by the hand of Pharaoh's daughter, no less. What's more, the mother was being asked to nurse her son. She could raise him in the faith of her forefathers, knowing that one day he would become a ruler of his people.

She had given her son to God, a slave's son condemned to die—He gave her son born again, a prince free to live.

His name was *Moses,* "one pulled from the water." (See Exodus 2.)

Moses—Man and Leader

Before them stretched the sea, a formidable force. Behind them the Egyptian army approached. Fear surged through them!

I can see Moses standing by the water, listening to the hearts of the people behind him hardening at the hopelessness of their situation. The grumbling continued incessantly: "You have sent us here to die! Didn't we tell you to let us stay in Egypt? It would have been better to serve the Egyptians than to die in the desert!"

I wonder if Moses thought about his childhood and how he had been pulled from the water. Every time someone called his name, he most probably remembered the Father's salvation in his life. "Hey Moses—*one pulled from the water*—have we come here to die?"

What a journey, what a path. Moses had traveled a lonely road, the road of faith. He had been raised up to be a leader of his people, but when his own heroic efforts failed, he ran—a wanted criminal, a rejected leader, fleeing his purpose, running, living in the wilderness of doubt.

Where was the Father? Why had He failed Moses? How would he ever be restored? What must he do to make it right? Questions roam your mind like caged lions, pushing you into a corner of self-doubt and fear, or bitterness and hatred. Then he met God at the burning bush. The Father spoke to Moses of His compassion for His people.

Compassion? After all these years?

The Father was calling Moses, now the failed leader, to lead his people. Moses' inadequacy rang out; his unbelief lashed out—he could not do it. Was there no one else?

But God was determined—Moses was the man. God was not worried about his inadequacy, only his doubt.

How Moses must have trembled as he returned to the great palace. He had left as a wanted criminal, fearing for his life. Now he must stand in front of the greatest emperor in the known world and demand that the pharaoh release God's people?

"Let My people go."
Refusal.
Plague.

"Let My people go."
Refusal.
Plague.

With each passing plague, the voice of the Lord through Moses grew louder; the hearts of the Egyptians grew harder. "Let My people go." Louder and louder. Ten plagues. Ten chances. Ten judgments.

At the cost of their firstborns, the Egyptians finally let the people go, begging them, paying them to go. "Please leave at once!" they pleaded, "May your God have mercy on us!"

The people of God departed with a conqueror's booty, slaves leaving with the wealth they had made for their masters. They journeyed into the wilderness, led by the spirit of God through a light-giving pillar of fire and a cloud of smoke. They finally made camp at the edge of the Red Sea. The stage was set.

Suffering from short-term memory loss, the Egyptians came, bearing down upon them in full rage. In fear the people of God grumbled and complained against their leader. But Moses knew what to do. He knew that God had been working and preparing His people for this one moment. There was only one place to go—the same place he had gone as a baby.

The "one pulled from the water," stretched out his hand, touched his staff to the sea, and parted it into dry land. The wind of God blew. The presence of the Father drew around them like a curtain, a father's arms around his child; they were cradled within His love.

They weren't just escaping; they were being immersed in the sea. As a child Moses had entered the water a slave and emerged a prince. The people entered the sea as slaves of Egypt, the black land, and emerge reborn as a nation of God called *Israel*—princes with God, destined to be a blessing to all nations in the world.

What rush of joy!
What songs they would sing!
God had rescued them,
By wind and fire they were free!

Here in the wilderness, the Father would shape this infant nation into a trusting child, delivering to them the children's edition of covenant love. Their name had a double meaning: the ones who wrestle with God. And wrestle they did, like a baby crying for attention until he learns that tears can be replaced with a simple request and humble obedience. The road from tears to trust is a pathway of learning.

Patiently the Father watered and fed them, tended to their needs and lovingly overlooked their selfish ways. But after a short distance, at the foot of a mountain, they were truly ready to meet the Father and begin their education, leaving ignorance for enlightenment.

Their world of darkness was soon to be illuminated by the life-giving light of the Father. Within the boundaries stood the mountain of Sinai, a place set apart—also called *holy*—where the Father would come and dwell.

It is love's nature to create a place that is set apart, where life can thrive. The Father created a planet with a delicately balanced ecosystem to allow life to thrive in an inhospitable universe. Love builds a house, a place where those who belong can live and grow under His watchful eye.

In the Kingdom of God, death is only the doorway to life. People of faith recognize it and embrace it. Those who live in doubt and unbelief not only reject the real life that God wants to offer them, but also embrace the harsh death of this present world; they are alive in body, but dead in spirit.

Fearful love

The fire of the Father's life-giving light fell on the mountain, veiled in a cloud of smoke that set the nation trembling for fear of their lives. The voice of the Father thundered from the cloud, causing the ground shake and their knees with it. The Father had come to dwell on the mountain.

Within the boundaries of the mountain was the Father's temporary dwelling place on earth. Inside this place set apart, Heaven reigned and nothing could stand within its borders unless granted by the Father. The tiny nation trembled at the sight. Where before they had only known ignorant darkness, now they saw the light of life, divine love burning like a fire. It threatened their existence because they were guilty of pursuing the fruit of sin and death. It made them aware that they were not set apart, but imperfect, because they were guilty of sin and death.

Could you stand before true divine love, an all-consuming fire burning with unending strength, perfect truth, and complete justice? Nothing can penetrate its walls and live unless love bids it to enter.

It is a fearful thing, this love. Many have faced this love and turned away, the price of it too great. Though they desired what it offered, yet they loved themselves too much.

> Though we may desire its light,
> are we willing to expose our darkness?
> Though we may desire its truth,
> are we willing to expose our deceptions?
> Though we may desire its strength,
> are we willing to expose our weakness?
> Though we may desire its life,
> are we willing to expose our death?
> Are we willing to face our fears?

Love would not end your fears, but right them. To come and stand in its light and gaze upon its strength will reveal every part of you. Like a refining fire it will burn away the rags of pride and your façades, the true nakedness of your soul and the miserable pain of your wanderings—and then clothe you in eternal radiance. This same fire that once kindled your greatest fears will become your greatest comfort. For the surrender of ourselves into its hands, love purifies us and perfects us, making us lovely. Truth and justice become our allied friends.

Love is to be greatly feared. If it were not, there would be no power in it. Yet this same danger that was once your foe becomes your friend, warning you of the only true danger left to you—separation from love itself.

For nothing in this world can separate us from love, except us...

Neither height nor depth
Nor angels nor principalities
Nor things present nor things to come.

Perhaps you find this sort of love difficult to follow, but love had simply turned on a light to make the truth clear. In our fallen condition, having rejected the life of the Father, we were pursuing the pathway of death. The Father is making our way clear, not to drive us away, but rather to drive us toward Him.

Love brings revelation of your weakness and need, in the light of its power and strength, so that you can take hold of its hope and find salvation from your death. This same fear that was now terrifying the fleeing infant nation would soon be their greatest comfort, assuring them of its protection from all injustice.

You have never really known God if you have never faced the truth of who He is, never realized the overwhelming power with which He holds the universe and judges all things, or acknowledged the fragility of your own existence. Do you know that if He should withhold His breath from you for merely an instance, you would be swept away for eternity? Any other image of God is an idol.

These things that now terrify you will set you free with overwhelming assurance when you are at peace within His dwelling. Fear of God is our pathway to knowing Him. You cannot approach Him until you recognize Him for who He is.

But the true fear of love is difficult for us to face. I imagine that if we saw love unveiled in all of its glory, our knees would give way, our voices would fail, and our hearts would freeze. So love, amazing love, crosses the bridge for us. It sends us a man of our own flesh and blood—an intercessor standing between infinite love and finite man that the two may be married.

The Promised Land in Sight

Moses—the humble man who spent 40 years wandering the wilderness learning about the Father; the man who met the Father in a burning bush and learned what it meant to stand on holy ground—would stand before the Father on behalf of the nation, and before the nation on behalf of the Father.

Entering the holy place and the smoky veil, he ascended the mountain until he was standing before the living fire; a meek man addressing the all-powerful Father, bearing upon his shoulders the weight of his people.

Just as the Father had covenanted to lead Abraham into the Promised Land, the Father was now going to covenant with His nation to lead them, too, into the Promised Land—if they followed Him obediently. But they were like children, ignorant in the ways of the Father. They did not understand how to follow Him and what it meant to live in His love.

This would be the children's edition of covenant.

As we learned through Abraham, covenant is usually based upon a stronger party promising to love—give life to—the other party. In response, the other party promises to trust and live in the love of their partner. Together they become as one through intimacy, having "knowledge" of each other. So, this infant nation had to learn what it meant to live in the life and love of the Father. Love had to become something practical for them until they understood what real love was.

The Father gave Moses the terms of their covenant. Quite simply, they had two basic commands:

- 🌿 To follow the love of the Father, and
- 🌿 To share this love with one another.

Covenant Love

Do any of us really know what love is? Has not the world warped this once beautiful and innocent fruit into deceptive opium of self-fulfillment that leads to death itself? Have not many tasted, through the world's love, the sweet poison of the forbidden fruit and lived in bitter agony of love and life lost?

We are helplessly lost in a world of love substitutes. Consider all that we apply the word *love* to and then ask, has it lost its true meaning? Do I believe the advertisements that tell me to apply this God-given gift to the latest car or hair care product? Will I really know love if I own this year's model? *Love* is merely a selfish word for what is good for me, by my definition.

By the Father's true love, He takes us from our self-love like children and educates us in real love. He leads us down the pathway of self-denial to true paradise. Along this road, growing up in love, we must enter the school of love and become its student. We must learn to let it live in us.

Thus the Father gave them Ten Commandments—five to teach them how to live in the Father's love and five to teach them how to live in each other's love. He gave them a lesson book of additional commandments to teach them how to apply the first ten. These were house rules, given to teach them how to practically live the ten rules and through them, the two greatest rules.

After meeting the Father, Moses returned to the base of the mountain and read the covenant to the nation. They agreed to follow it and Moses, on their behalf, made a covenant with the

Father. He sealed the covenant by sacrificing a bull, a token of their lives and possessions.

Moses took the blood of the animal, the symbol of its life, and sprinkled part of it on the altar and part of it on the people. This action symbolized that they were receiving the life of the Father, and that the Father was receiving theirs, too, as the blood entered the fire—the symbol of the Father's life-giving light. The nation and the Father were one, married in unity, He promising to house-band them and they promising to trust in His love.

Moses returned to the mountaintop to meet with the Father again. There the Father finalized their covenant promise in stone tablets—the tablets of testimony, an eternal proof that their relationship had been consummated.

Now the Father would begin the process of reshaping His nation around the covenant. Everything they did would be in celebration and remembrance of it.

At the Father's instruction they prepared a chest to hold and embody the covenant agreement. It was fashioned from wood and covered with gold, their most valuable commodity, which signified the highest level of holiness. The chest held their most set-apart items: the testimony of the covenant and its handbook, the *Book of the Law*.

On top of the chest they placed a cover called the mercy seat, to show that the Father's merciful love would protect their covenant and all those who were part of it. Symbolically, the entire nation was inside the chest. Upon the seat of mercy they sprinkled the blood of a bull, the symbol of their life resting upon the mercy of the Father. Above the chest stood two cherubim, wings spread together at the top, a symbol of living creation in its fullest beauty. Between the cherubim, the life-giving fire of the Father in purest form, the *Shekinah,* would come and dwell, to show that He was the center of all, the source of all life. From the mercy seat, the Father hovered over their marriage covenant, giving life to it as He gave life to the living creatures.

The Ark of the Covenant was placed inside the Tent of Testimony, the dwelling place of the Father. Here, He would teach them what it meant to dwell with Him in covenant love.

The Father didn't need a house to live in; He had Heaven as His home. But He wanted to create a house for His children—to spend time with them, teaching them how to live, showing them what it was like to dwell with Him, to learn to trust Him.

Children play with toys, symbols of real life, practicing what they see their parents doing, and placing themselves in an imaginary world to learn about being grown up. They watch first, then do, and then by doing, learn to understand why afterward. The tabernacle was a playhouse for the nation. There they watched the priests act out symbolically how to dwell with the Father.

Love teaches us to act and follow and by following we don't just *act* love, we *become* love. For the people, no symbol better taught them about love than a covenant and no picture better captured a covenant than a house.

But this was only a temporary house. Someday they would outgrow this place and something much greater would replace it—love itself.

Looking across the nation in the crisp morning air he saw smoke rising, the exhalation of campfires scattered through out the barren valley. Next to them the Jordan River snaked through the valley down toward the Dead Sea, the lowest place on earth. Across the river stood the bulk of the land that the Father had promised to them. A place flowing with milk and honey. But more than a river was separating them from their homeland.

It had taken them 40 years to reach this point and Moses, now at 120 years old, was the last of his generation. His time on earth was drawing short.

The people of God, numbering over 600,000, had been transformed from a mere crowd of slaves into a well organized nation with laws, a judicial system, environmental practices, customs, and rituals. Their entire life, culture, and encampment centered around the dwelling place of the Father, the tabernacle. Moses saw smoke, too, rising from the tabernacle, the exhalation of the morning sacrifices from the brass altar.

Everything was based upon the celebration of their covenant. When they sinned or rebelled, celebrated or rejoiced, they always came to the altar to bring an offering in remembrance of their covenant.

By the covenant blood, they became holy. It was nothing of their own, only the mercy of the Father to forgive them of their sin and to make them His holy possession. It was by the laws that they lived within the covenant. When they fell short of the laws, they returned again to the altar, returned again to the covenant, to find holiness in their Father and husband. They always came with a perfect animal, the symbol of a pure heart's desire to be in unity with the Father. They laid their hand upon its head, to show that they were placing their life upon it; then it was drained of its life and the blood married with the fire. It was painful to see the cost of sin in the loss of life, but liberating to be restored again to the life of the Father.

But they also came to bring an offering of celebration to thank Him for His love. After they had made their offering, they could stand in the courts and ponder the Father's house. The house was tended by a patriarch, a father—the chief priest—and his family. This family represented a tribe called Levi, *ones joined with God.*

The family could only enter into the house after being immersed in a brass bath. As they entered into the bath, the hot desert sun reflected a beautiful golden light upon them to signify that they had died to their old life to be born again into the life of the Father.

The entrance into the tent was draped so that only family members could see or enter into its life. This was a private affair; those outside would know by the priests' word what it was actually like to dwell in the Father's house.

Passing beyond the curtain the priests entered the set-apart place and beheld the sights and smells of the home. On the right side of the room was the *table of the face* and upon it the 12 loaves of bread, the symbol of the Father's fellowship with the 12 tribes of the nation. Through it the nation would learn that their strength came from seeking the face of the Lord and finding His counsel.

On the left side of the room, a warm glow emanated from the *seven-candled lamp stand.* In seven days, the Father brought the world from nothing into fullness of life. Over time, those who dwelt in the tabernacle would grow in fullness of life and perfect understanding. By the light of the Father's wisdom, they would learn to walk and would ultimately reach the source of life itself, at the far end of the home.

There in front of them was a veil, and in front of the veil was the altar of incense. Upon this altar burned the hot coals from the altar outside and upon the coals burned incense, filling the room with a pleasant fragrance.

At the altar outside, the smell of death abounded, but here in the place of dwelling with the Father, the fire brought a fragrant smell of life. Thus, to the outside world, the sacrifice of life is repugnant—yet to those dwelling in the Father's love and to the Father Himself it is the smell of life. The smoke not only filled the room, but rose through the veil from the Holy Place to the innermost chamber, the Holiest Place.

They could not yet see the Holiest Place, but they believed in the place where the real presence of the Father dwelt in all His fullness, the place where their covenant was kept safely hidden— Heaven. Standing between them and Heaven was the veil of finite mortality.

Only once a year could the high priest, their intercessor, enter the Holiest Place to renew the covenant by sprinkling fresh blood upon the seat. Here again, the nation was reminded of their dependency upon one to stand between them and the Father, to bring the truth to them and to bring them, by the blood of life, to the Truth.

At the pain of death, the Ark of the Covenant was guarded by the life-giving light of the Father. The same presence that shook the mountain of Sinai and had threatened their death before, now fiercely guarded their marriage covenant. What had been their greatest fear was now their greatest comfort.

This was the smoke of the living fire that bellowed up through the roof of the tabernacle and into the sky where Moses could see it from his distant viewpoint outside the camp.

Just like their journey into the desert, the tabernacle was a model of how the nation had come to the Father through a baptism in the sea into new life, how they were nourished with bread from Heaven and were brought into the fullness of understanding by the light of His presence. And there they dwelt with the Father by the altar, the smoke of their prayerful offerings filling the camp and rising through the veil of the sky into Heaven as a pleasant fragrance and continual reminder of their covenant marriage.

Deadly doubt

Two silver trumpets blew forth a call.

The serpent despised the love of the Father, hated His kindness, detested His mercy. Deceptively he crept through the camp, whispering into their ears. "Does He really love you?" "Will He really care for you?" "Can you really trust Him?"

Their doubts took root and grew into grumbling, their grumbling into rebellion. And their rebellion brought sadness, deep sadness to the heart of Moses and even more, to the heart of the Father. A stubborn unbelieving nation, oh how easily they forgot His love and power.

Now overlooking the Jordan River, Moses could remember how, many years before, he had stood here with them on the edge of the wilderness and had been forced to turn away—because of their fears, because they doubted the love of the Father.

He had parted the red sea,
and they were afraid.
He had destroyed the Egyptian
armies, and they were afraid.
He had met with them on the
mountain, and they were afraid.
He had fed them,
and they were afraid.

They spent 40 years in the wilderness, doubting and complaining—they had even built an idol and worshiped it. Their Bridegroom had come and delivered them from Egypt. This tiny insignificant nation was His chosen maiden. Yet only weeks after crossing the Red Sea, while Moses was meeting with God on the mountain, they built an idol.

The Father's children worshiped an image of a cow made by their own hands! His anger burned against them. He was ready to destroy them. But Moses pled for his people. He loved them and so did God.

But lest I judge them in hypocrisy, I am forced to look back on my own life with painful regret. I spent many years wandering in the wilderness of doubt and despair. God had called me to come to the mountain and meet with Him. Instead I doubted the love of the Father.

Seeds of doubt took root in my mind, and then grew into weeds that clouded my thoughts. I tried to fight against them, but grumbling and complaining took over.

"The Lord has forgotten me."
"Where are His promises?"
"Why are You distant from me, oh God?"
"Why have You left me here?"

In my doubts and grumbling I turned to disobedience, depending on my own strength. Yet the more I tried to remedy my despair, the more difficulty I found. Debt increased, failure increased, sorrow increased. Perhaps as Moses stood looking toward the Promised Land, he remembered the years he had spent in the wilderness before God called him out. Because of his own doubts and disillusionment, he had taken pity on the people for their doubts. The Father would have taken no pleasure in destroying them; but if Moses had not been willing to carry their responsibility, they would have been worse off wandering in the wilderness, thanking a golden calf for delivering them from Egypt.

Moses had rescued them from His judgment, bringing them back to the Father, bringing them back to His mercy and to repentance.

Now, Moses was ready to share with them his final words. His end was near. He had shepherded these people for 40 years and he was the last of his generation. All others had died in the wilderness due to their unbelief. Moses himself would have to die here too. Most of the members of the camp he looked upon had been mere children when they left Egypt.

Moses exhorted them to be strong and courageous, to not make the mistake of the older generation. He urged them to obediently trust in the love of the Father to fulfill His promises and lead them into the Promised Land.

How it must have broken his heart to think that someday this new generation might also forget the covenant. Would they cross the Jordan, enter the Promised Land, become comfortable in their lives, and forget the Father? Would they forget the covenant and the life that it promised? Would they forget about the wilderness and the Red Sea? Would they return to slavery? Oh, it would not be Egypt, but they would become slaves to another nation, a nation that would despise and mock them.

The Father had led Moses to the top of a great mountain. From there he could see across the Jordan and into the land he had desired for his entire life. He could imagine great towns and villages—children playing, women dancing, men rejoicing—the prosperity of the Father abounding. And the nations of the world would come to inquire how this was possible.

The nations would someday come and seek the love of their God, the great Father. But for Moses, his time on earth was ended. It was time to cross the real Jordan, leaving this world to enter into the real Promised Land, and in it the Father's house.

One day, I look forward to meeting him there.

CHAPTER FIVE

Land of Hope

*A*n *old wooden door* opens and the feet of a woman once beautiful, now tired looking, descend a dry, stone staircase to join the river of people moving along the street below. Seeing with hopeless eyes she follows the road down to the main gate and out of the city, a formidable city, where she can look back at her home, built into the wall of Jericho.

Down this road she walks…must walk…every day. Then she waits for a prince in tarnished armor, a knight for a night. Who cares, really, as long as he pays her?

This was work to Rahab, the daily grind. This was life. To Jericho and the land in which she lived there was no sacredness in marriage. Love was just an emotion, a momentary thrill—one that put food on Rahab's table and clothed her family.

How many walk this same road? How many bare their souls for a moment of illusionary love, offering what can't be returned—dying one step, one day at a time?

Why Does the Father Hate Sin?

On the mountain of Sinai, the Father spoke to Moses about three types of sin:

The first, *stumbling*. Quite simply a mistake. There may be a number of reasons for it, but it is all related to our shortfall of life, our dependency on self that keeps us from living in the perfect life of the Father. When woman took the fruit in the garden at the serpent's temptation, she was deceived and therefore guilty only of stumbling.

The second, *rebellion*, is when we purposely step outside of the Father's love and life to fulfill our own desires. The only difference between stumbling and rebellion is that man *intentionally* rebels. When man took the fruit in the garden he was not deceived; therefore, he was guilty of rebellion because he knew the truth.

The third is *warping*—or as some translate, *iniquity*—when we warp the truth to create deception, bringing death not only to ourselves, but also to those around us. When the serpent deceived woman, he was guilty of this level because he caused her to stumble; he was responsible for her death.

The warped are taken most seriously by the Father because, not content to merely rebel in their own desires, they infect others with their deception, which spreads like a cancer through society and destroys love in the name of love. Children are born into a world of pain and misery.

Rahab's land was ruled by warping…and its offspring: worldly fear, oppression, selfishness, and hatred.

Her people rejected the Father. They sacrificed children—for their own emotional pleasure, they sacrificed children. Innocence was destroyed before it was understood.

In the Western world we sacrifice our unborn for nothing more than our own comfort and pleasure. We call it "choice." The act is *warped* in the eyes of the Father who lovingly crafted every child ever conceived throughout history.

But not even "choice" can compare to bringing a child—born into your household, whom you have named, and fed, and clothed—to the temple, looking into innocent eyes, handing the child to the temple priests, then watching coldly while your child is mercilessly put to death, is a particular brand of evil. One life is destroyed for another's moment of warped pleasure.

We may feel deep grief and sorrow to imagine such darkness. But our grief is only a mere fraction of the pain felt by the Father who created every child with the same hope and purpose that He placed in Adam and Eve at the beginning.

The Father, in His mercy, has limited our emotional capacity. We can feel pain and grief, joy and happiness, but only to a degree. But imagine living as an infinite immortal able to feel unlimited emotion. For living in truth means living truthfully in your emotions: in pain that cannot be ignored, in anger that must be answered. The Creator of finite human emotion will not rationalize away His infinite divine emotions.

He will not harden His heart!

Another Way

Looking up, Rahab met the gaze of two travelers entering her city. Her heart stopped for a moment. *Maybe the rumors were true,* she thought. She smiled with all the warmth she could muster and beckoned them. "You gentlemen look tired. How about a place to rest?"

The men followed her into the city, up the steps and into her apartment on the city wall. They were disinterested in her services, her alluring clothes, and her broken smile. They weren't heeding her tempting glances or the dancing of her painful eyes.

Instead their eyes carefully surveyed the city, mentally photographing every image: gates and guards, streets, and shops. They quietly studied every detail and subtly noticed every person.

But Rahab wasn't the only one who noticed their arrival. Word reached the network of guards and moved up through the ranks to the King. These men were spies of the people in the wilderness, not welcome here. Soldiers were dispatched to find them.

As Rahab watched the men she wondered—was it all true?

A people who worshiped one God?
A God who rescued them from slavery?
A God who fed them in the wilderness?
A God who would inhabit no
image made by human hands?
Could such a God exist?
Could He be her God?

She knew it was true. She saw in their eyes quiet confidence, hope shining forth, virtue deep and pure. Her soul was drawn to them; their life warmed the coldness of her heart like sunshine in winter. She knew they were people from a different land. She had heard of them; all of Jericho had. Word traveled from mouth to mouth, fear traveled from ear to ear. The entire city knew of these people and trembled. Now they were here, in her house. It was true!

What would she do? Time was against her, beating down upon her; it would not wait for her to think. The sun could not stand still. The soldiers would come; she knew it.

If she handed over the spies...perhaps a reward. The town would be in her debt. But how long would it last? How long till she was back on that cursed street again? And what of the others like these men? Would they come to avenge their deaths?

She held their lives in her hands; they trusted her.

The same battle that Rahab faced every day rages more loudly today—to believe in true love or not, to pursue life or not. These are moments when the same daily decision stops being a daily decision. The future rises up to confront you and says it's not just for now—it's forever.

The voice that she had tried to silence, her conscience, now shouted at her. God was speaking to her. If she betrayed the spies, she betrayed her heart, and Him.

What little life was left to beat within her was fighting to be heard. Show them mercy...and hope, hope for something different.

But what hope for her? What would they give her? Perhaps more than prostitution. Perhaps a gesture of mercy. Perhaps a kind master. Perhaps...no...no, it was too much to hope for a husband, a covenant, and love. A real life.

The pounding on the door was echoed in her heart.

"Open!" the Jericho soldiers shouted. But her heart was open. The soldiers were rushing in, searching for the spies, but she had hidden them.

"Where are they?" they shouted.

"Gone from here," she whispered. The soldiers looked throughout the house but, thankfully, not carefully enough. Then they scrambled out the old wooden door and down the stone steps to search the next home.

That night after the city gates were closed, Rahab hung a crimson rope out her window and lowered the men down along the wall. They had completed their mission, but not before promising to spare Rahab and her family upon their return to Jericho. Returning to Joshua, the spies reported their experience in Jericho.

As they left, Rahab's eyes filled with hope. Her faith was marvelous. She hadn't crossed the Red Sea, stood at the mountain, or eaten the bread of Heaven, yet she believed. She believed in that nation enough to risk her life and everything that she had known, to be a part of it.

Moses had commanded the people to spare no one when they entered the Promised Land. It was so dark with evil that it had to be wiped clean. But because this woman had shown incredible love to the spies, the Father would show the same love to her.

Another Sight

His name was different then: Hoshea, meaning "he will deliver," and deliver he did. He fought battles valiantly. As Moses' faithful assistant, he had earned the rank of captain and the trust of the great leader.

The first time the Israelites approached the Promised Land, Moses named Hoshea as one of 12 spies sent to spy the land. What fear, what darkness he felt on the other side of the Jordan: imposing giants, fortified cities, and ruthless rulers. He could feel the hopelessness of the land falling in on him; the demons pursuing him, taunting, "Is your God really with you?"

But of the 12, only Hoshea and one other spy, Caleb, believed in the Father to be their strength and to fight for them. The serpent then turned his efforts on the other ten spies casting darkness into their souls through his cold unbelieving eyes. They hardened their hearts and under his taunting breath incited the people to try stoning Hoshea and Caleb to death.

Those in darkness hate the light; it's a searing pain upon their closed eyes.

The reports of the ten doubting spies infected the camp with such fear and terror that Hoshea and Caleb were hard pressed to counter it. This unbelief brought 40 years of wandering to the Father's people until Moses and those infected with the disease passed away. It was up to the next generation to take the land.

Hoshea's true courage and belief in the Father earned him a new name, Joshua, meaning "God will deliver." Joshua was determined not to let the covenant between God and his forefathers die. After all, Moses had reminded them again and again:

> Be strong and courageous!
> Be strong and courageous!
> Be strong and courageous!

A New Day

That day, as Joshua and Caleb surveyed the camp, they realized that they alone of their generation had survived. That day, it was time for them to cross the Jordan and enter the Promised Land. That day, a new generation of warriors would consecrate themselves to God through the same spiritual baptism Moses' generation had in the Red Sea.

Today, we have the opportunity to cross the Jordan and leave the wilderness. We have the opportunity to leave unbelief behind and enter into the true promised land of holiness by faith.

The Jordan, meaning "the descender," was a river winding down a valley and flowing into the Dead Sea, the lowest point on earth. Trying to ford the river at this time of year, the time of harvest was certain death. The river flooded its banks and became too deep to cross on foot.

The priests went in front of the camp carrying the Ark of the Covenant, and with it the promises of the Father; and with the promises, the presence of the Father Himself.

Just as Moses had gone before his followers asking the Father to open the Red Sea, now Moses' covenant was going before them, not only parting the river, but also cutting off the entire flow at a distant upstream town called *Adam.* As the covenant entered the river, the water dried up, and the Father carried His people into their new land. The Bridegroom carried His Bride across the threshold of their new home.

The Father's merciful love cut off the flow of death from Adam, making a way for those who believe to cross into the land of promise, through a baptism into new life, leaving behind the reproach of death.

Upon reaching the other side, Joshua ordered 12 stones to be brought up out of the Jordan and placed in a circle as a monument to how God had brought the 12 tribes into the land and set them free. In this place known as *Gilgal,* or "circle," Joshua commanded the people of God to circumcise themselves in recommitment to the covenant, because none of those born in the wilderness had been circumcised.

Just as Abram covenanted with the Father, once using animals and the second time using his own heart, so this nation had covenanted the first time using animals at Sinai and renewing the covenant with their hearts through circumcision. The first covenant taught them about the love of the Father and brought them to the second covenant, which was written on their hearts. If the first was like a wedding ceremony, the second was a consummation truly entering into the covenant.

It was only in the second baptism, bringing them to the second covenant, that their slavery was truly rolled away and they became the nation of Israel. Like the Levites at the brass bath, they had truly been immersed into new life and now were free to enter into the house that Love had prepared for them—the Promised Land.

A New Battle

Joshua slipped out of the camp at night and walked toward Jericho. In the distance, silhouetted against the night sky was a man with a sword drawn for battle. Joshua's mind went on the defensive: *Whom does he work for? Which side is he on? Is he friend or foe? Should I fight or flee?*

"Are you for us or for our enemies?" he asked.

"Neither," the man responded, "but as commander of the army of the Lord, I have now come." (See Joshua 5:13-14.)

Today it is the same. The Lord takes the side of no man. The Lord *is* the side. His plan. His purpose. His world. His life. Are you for Him, or against Him? Are you for life or for death? Are you for light or are you for darkness? There is no middle road.

The commander of the Lord's army laid before Joshua a war plan. The Israelites were to circle Jericho with the Ark of the Covenant for seven days, once a day on the first six days and seven times on the last day. The trumpeters were to go before them, but they were to make no war cries until the blast of the final trumpet on the final day. Then, and only then, would the city be delivered into their hands.

From Rahab's window, she could watch the people of God marching around the city wall, the trumpeters first, then the Ark of the Covenant. Nervous tension filled the city and now she thought of the role she had played in what was happening today. Her fears played upon her emotions; her emotions played upon her mind.

> The trumpeters blew. The people marched.
> Would they remember her?
> The trumpeters blew. The people marched.
> Would they spare her life?
> The trumpeters blew. The people marched.
> Would they spare her family?
> The trumpeters blew. The people marched.
> Would they be kind to her?
> The trumpeters blew. The people marched.
> Who was their God?
> The trumpeters blew. The people marched.
> Would He show her love?

On the seventh day they marched their final circle, a consecration to God, a sacrifice. At His command everything in Jericho would belong to God, dedicated to His treasury and His service.

Trumpets blow. People shout. The earth quakes. Walls crumble and fall. People rush. The city trembles. Guards fall. The warped are defeated. The city is on fire and its treasure is gone. It is a sacrifice to God.

At the time of harvest, Jericho became the firstfruits of the land, an offering to the Father. Everything within its walls belonged to Him: gold, silver, bronze, livestock, and clothing.

But of all the treasures offered to the Lord that day, the greatest was a prostitute who believed in the Father. The loving Father plucked His child from the mud and washed her clean. He would redeem her womb in a way that would bring His love to the entire world.

Her faith was a treasure glowing in the eyes of the Lord.

To the dirty, the lonely, the abused, the lost, the poor, and the desperate: blessed are you, for the Kingdom of Heaven is waiting for you. No greater gift can you offer than your faith!

I Deserve It

"Take it," the serpent whispered in his ear. Achan, whose name means "the troubler," looked around. "Take it," the serpent whispered again as Achan looked upon the gold and silver with lustful desire. "You deserve it."

Achan knew the word of the Lord. Jericho was God's sacrifice; it all belonged to Him. But, reaching out his hand, he hardened his heart. "I deserve it."

And the sacrifice of God had been desecrated. (See Joshua 1–7.)

The nation had entered the Father's house, come to His table and found that His strength was theirs. The city was laid bare before them simply because they had followed His counsel. They were surrounded with victory, without lifting a sword, because they had sought His face.

Only His life, His face, His counsel can sustain you.

When you approach Him in holy fear and come to know Him in intimacy, He brings you, by His counsel, to the table of His provision and says, "Feast with Me." When you remove your rags and approach Him in naked honesty, He clothes you with His robes and sets you by His fire to warm your soul. Every need He tenderly meets as you seek His face.

As we approach love in fear, it brings us into knowledge. Knowledge teaches us to seek His intimate counsel, and by His counsel we find His strength. Fear, knowledge, counsel, and strength.

But we have to keep returning to Him—returning to His place of covenant and life. A one-night stand is not good enough. Remember His love. Remember His covenant. Return to *Gilgal*—"the circle"—the Father's circle of life.

Oh, those who forget to return! They fight the battles of life alone. They face the enemy exposed. They start in faith, but then faith wanes; its glow leaves their hearts.

The enemy presses in. Fear presses in. They drown in a sea of whys. They blame love for leaving them…when they are the ones who left love.

Love pleads: Do not forget the place where He set you free. Do not stop returning to Him for true freedom and victory. In His eyes, His beautiful eyes, life is found. His smile warms your soul, fills you with faith, and encourages you to hope.

The priests returned every day. They washed their hands and feet in the bath, washed away their selves, and entered into His house to celebrate the covenant again.

When you go back to Gilgal and consecrate yourself to Him, returning to the dwelling of holiness, He will fill you with faith and send you out. Great battles He will fight for you, great victories will be won. But first, go back, go back and lay yourself before Him. Go back and consecrate yourself to the Father again, return to His holy place and dwell in His house.

Go Back

Great fear struck the people of God. Terror filled their hearts. Word reached Joshua that the soldiers had returned defeated. Thirty-six lay dead along the road.

Where are You, God? Were You not with us yesterday when we defeated Jericho? You brought the walls down. You filled our souls with hope!

Now, the enemy will destroy us. He will come to us while we are weak. Why were we defeated? Why did You not deliver Ai? It was a small village. Why could we not take it? The whys were closing in on the minds.

Joshua wept. He cried out to the Lord. The whole nation cried out. They were ready to retreat. They were willing to return back to the wilderness of doubt. Joshua was on his face, hiding himself in fear.

"Get up!" the voice from Heaven spoke. They had not returned to Gilgal in their hearts; they had not gone back to seek the Lord. In the joy of their victory, they had moved on, without stopping to seek His counsel and find His strength.

Sin entered the camp. Sin allowed defeat.

When they did not go back to Gilgal in their hearts, when they did not remember, when they did not consecrate, Egypt began to fill their hearts again and idols took up residence. Their strength failed.

But the bread of His counsel is everlasting. It filled their souls again and restored their strength. We, as they, must always go back to Gilgal and seek His face. We, as they, must go back and renew ourselves before Him again. We, as they, must be faithful to seek Him continually; for it is His battle, and it is His victory.

Joshua was exhaling his last breaths. Soon his spirit would depart and be carried into Heaven on the almighty wind of God. Under the Father's perfect counsel, the Israelites had done great things. They had possessed the land.

But as Joshua's life on earth was waning, the people's hearts were turning again toward the idols. He knew their disobedience would cost them dearly. When the strength of the Father retreated, the serpent would return.

"Why must you not taste it?" he had hissed at Adam and Eve. "It is beautiful. Look at it." He closed in upon them. "Give in to your desires." His breath was cold and its stench foul, but intoxicating.

Remember Gilgal.

Remember.

CHAPTER SIX

City of Peace

*M*usical notes floated upward, from harp strings to the heavens and into the Father's house, carried on a gentle wind to His very ears. The sound brought great joy to Heaven, the sound of a praiseful heart.

With simplicity he laid his life before the king of Heaven. With joy his soul became a living offering. With purity of heart and strength of voice he sang.

The Father's love shone into David's heart, filling it like liquid sunshine. The love poured through David and into the tiny flock of sheep that he shepherded faithfully, their gentle bleats blended as a choir, accompanying his sweet melody.

The Father loved His creation, every small detail. David knew it, could feel it. What strength and power flowed through him the day the bear growled, or the night the lion prowled! The power of God's love overtook his fear and overwhelmed him with courage. How else could this young teenager single-handedly kill the wild beasts, were it not for the courage of the Lord?

But now, his notes filled the air and joy filled his heart. He was lost in the presence and pure joy of the Father. The Father was pleased with this young shepherd; joy filled His heart at the sound of David's voice. It was time to show David the greatness of His pleasure.

"David," his brother called to him. "David, come home; you have been called to a feast."

David left his sheep and went to the house. The prophet and priest, Samuel, meaning, "heard from God," stood before him. He could see in his eyes, the joy of the Lord. He could see hope, but the hope was shining on him, David.

Samuel had heard from the Father and bent over David to empty the contents of his horn upon him. Fragrant oil fell upon David's head, down his face, and onto his shoulders, arms and hands. His lungs were filled with the fragrance of the oil—but more than that, the fragrance of Heaven, and the fragrance of the Father's pleasure. The Father had heard David's heart song.

Anointing oil enters life as a bitter fruit. When ripe, the olives are picked and crushed with bitter spices. Together, what was lonely and bitter is crushed into something unified and sweet.

The same elements that fill the tabernacle—the oil bringing light and understanding, the spices that flavor the bread and the incense that burns fragrantly upon the altar—are blended together, to anoint the priests, surrounding them with the fragrance of their home. It is a symbol of the Spirit of love. It blends the elements of the covenant into one substance that brings a pleasant life to all those around.

To those who dwell in the Father's house, it is a gift to them, to carry the fragrant life of the house with them into the world and bring the covenant of true love to men, and to bring men to the covenant of true love.

The hallmark of an anointed one is the heart of worship. *Worship means to prostrate yourself, completely surrendered to the purpose of the Father.* To be completely emptied of yourself, that you may be completely filled with Him; the fullness of love covering you and invisibly touching all those around you with the intoxicating power of its fragrance.

Thus, an anointed one is one who has the love of Heaven bestowed upon him. And David, *the beloved one,* had been given this gift. The Father had set him apart for something greater, much greater than shepherding sheep. David would shepherd His people. He would be their king. The young boy from Bethlehem, "the house of bread," would be the Father's means of strength for a hungry and weak nation.

Someday. Someday.

David went back to tending his sheep.

Step, Sacrifice, Worship, Praise

The Ark moved at a slow pace up the long, winding road—the thrill of worship building in David's heart. Many had come to watch the procession. His calling was about to be fulfilled, marking the end of a long and difficult period in the nation's history.

How God's people had wandered. They had grumbled against Him in the wilderness. They had turned against him in the Promised Land. They had forgotten His love, His presence, and His strength. They had forgotten Him.

Their spiritual adultery had brought great disappointment to the Father, but He gave them what they asked for. They served other gods and other people. They lived in fear, misery, and death. The giants of the land closed in upon them—oppressed them, raided their villages, and stole their possessions. The people wept. They had forgotten the covenant; and the Ark, its symbol, had been removed from them and held by the nation they feared.

But the Father never forgot them. He was still protecting the covenant and the Ark, even in the presence of their enemies. Though they were out from under His covenant, yet His covenant promises were still alive. He could lead them. He could rescue them. He could save them—if only they would trust in Him. But they didn't want Him, they wanted a man.

They had a covenant with God Almighty, yet they wanted a king.

In the beginning, the Father had spoken to them through judges. Judges are counselors. They can advise, they can judge, but they cannot rule. It is up to people to decide if they will follow. In effect, Israel was a democracy. They "did what was right in their own eyes," inquiring of the Father only when they thought they needed Him.

Though the Father desired to be much more than a counselor and judge to them, they desired nothing more. They wanted a human king and this broke the Father's heart. They could have been the only nation on the face of the planet with the Father as their king, but they wanted a human king instead.

He gave them what they asked for. His name was Saul, *the one asked for,* a strong, valiant, courageous, handsome, wise, human king. But Saul forgot. Just as the people forgot to inquire of the Father and did what was right in their own eyes, so Saul forgot. And when Saul went to Gilgal to fight a war, he forgot. He forgot the lesson that his nation had learned there; instead, he proceeded without the counsel of the Lord. He forgot Gilgal. And he lost the right to the crown.

Why, oh people of God, do you forget?

He sends you bread from heaven and you forget? He carries you into the Promised Land and you forget? He calls you His own, and you forget? But then, so do I.

One Who Remembers

David was a simple, humble, faithful shepherd—one whom the Father could love, one who could love a nation. Just like the Ark, David, too, had traveled a long and winding road. He was just a boy when Samuel drenched him with oil, just a boy in those green pastures dotted with sheep. David spent many years spent in the wilderness—running, hiding, fighting, and fleeing Saul's jealous desire for his murder.

Many times David could have killed Saul, but he didn't. He remembered that the Father had anointed Saul and that it was the Father who would remove him.

In the wilderness, while David was hiding for his life, while his soul was being crushed by his trials, the sheep gathered. Straggly sheep. They were a motley band of discontented debtors who wanted a shepherd. They smelled the fragrance of Heaven's love upon David and knew that there was life in him, regardless of his appearance. The anointing of Heaven touched them through David, and brought them into life, even though they lived as fugitives in a desert.

There's nothing wrong with feeling discontentment with this world. There's everything right with it. Discontentment tells us that the world's values aren't right, that life can be better, that we're not happy with what the world offers, that we're not fulfilling our purpose. It is a hunger in the stomach of our hearts.

How do you feed the hunger in your heart? Do you live in famine and pretend that you're not hungry? Or do you look for food, real food, food that satisfies?

It broke this shepherd's heart to see his nation like sheep without a shepherd, hungry and viciously oppressed by enemies. And what shepherd can stand to see sheep unprotected and exposed to the wolves of the world? Oh, that they would come and eat at the Father's table and be full. Oh, that they would feast on His presence and taste and see that He is good. That He will feed their weakness with His strength.

With the true heart of a shepherd, David laid down his life for the sheep. He made himself a brother to them. He covenanted with them, and in so doing showed them how to covenant with the Father. This is the way of anointing; it comes by unity. David learned how to dwell in unity with the Father through worship, the sacrifice of the heart. He made himself a brother to others and taught them how to dwell in unity with him, with each other, and with the Father. David filled them with the fragrant anointing oil of Heaven, the spirit of love. In the same way Moses stood before the nation on Sinai, David was standing before the Father on their behalf, teaching them to love the Father.

And out of those who were truly discontent with this world, who were weak and hungry, brokenhearted and poor, he formed an army of the most fearful warriors. The Father took weaklings and made them strong in His love, using the humble servant heart of a shepherd, the anointed one, to bring them life.

This is the Father's idea of a king, one who lays down his life for his nation; one who is anointed with the fragrant spirit of divine love to bring the people into the spirit of love by teaching them how to covenant. A true king does not force his dominion upon others. He simply offers it and those who truly desire it will find it.

In a sense, an anointed one is like a walking, breathing, living tabernacle, carrying the presence of the Father within and teaching, by example, what it means to live in covenant with the Father. The anointed one is a living, burning message.

David's dominion grew from a band of warriors to a tribe until eventually the entire nation came to seek him as their king. Saul, the self-dependent, self-seeking king was removed and the beloved one replaced him.

The nation was completely surrendered to a man who was completely surrendered to the Father. The Father Himself was now their king through a human representative. This is what the Father desired through Adam, to lovingly bring the world to life through a trusting son.

The Ark Advances

By the Father's counsel and strength, David had liberated the wrestlers from their oppressors and built them a home, a place of protection, a city. The city imagined by Abraham. Jerusalem, the City of David was a city on a hill, a place of worship and refuge, and the living expression of David's heart. As the people surrendered to the heart of David, this city would become the heart of the nation.

Returning the Ark brought the covenant back to the heart of the nation. With each step, David made a sacrifice, creating a pathway of lifeblood for the covenant to come to the city—just as

David's own life had been a sacrifice, a pathway for the covenant to come to the heart of the nation.

The presence of the Father and the Ark of His covenant entered the city gates. Sacrificial step by sacrificial step, the covenant ascended the hill. There were worship, offering, praise, joy, and celebration.

The Ark, carried on the priests' shoulders, reached the top of the hill and was placed at rest in a new home—a new tabernacle—different from the tabernacle of Moses.

From this day forward, the people of the Father could look toward the city and find inspiration. They could come to find His presence, peace, safety, and security—just like David did all those years ago, worshiping the Father among the sheep. He would teach them to worship, sacrificing themselves unto the Lord. They would leave His presence with thankfulness on their lips, declaring the beauty of God. They would go through the land singing His praise. The joy would be infectious. All the tribes would come and worship. All this would take place under the watchful eye of their good shepherd, David—who was himself watched by the eye of the Shepherd of the universe.

The covenant was again in the heart of a home in the heart of a nation.

David clothed in kingly glory, in awe of the Father's immense beauty, humbled by His blessings, and overjoyed at His faithfulness, stripped himself of his robes; and, humbled in his nakedness, worshiped the Father and danced for joy in His love. David's greatest act of worship; his glory, his dignity, his city, his people, all belonged to the Father.

A Permanent Home

His eyes were growing dim, his body growing cold. But he could still clearly remember that day when he brought the Ark to Jerusalem and to the tent of worship. The Father's people were prospering under His blessing. But it wasn't enough.

He wanted to do more for the Father. Worship is addictive.

He remembered looking upon that tent with conviction strong upon his heart. Why should the Father be in a tent, a temporary dwelling, while David himself lived in a palace?

Perhaps the Father would allow him to build a permanent house. Maybe he could erect a glorious monument to the Father in worship that not only His people, but also the people of the world would come to see.

But the Father said no.

David was a man of war and bloodshed. Though the Father loved him dearly, His temple would be a place where peace was made with the Father. David was not suitable for this task. But if David could not build the temple, he could prepare for it, so that his son, Solomon, the prince of peace, could build it.

David's request, his unending love for God, pleased Him. "My home is all of heaven, earth is only My footstool. How can you build a house for Me? I don't need a house built by you, but I will build your house, David. Forever your house shall stand; forever your descendents shall reign. One is coming from you whose throne will be forever." (See Isaiah 66:1.)

The Father's response overwhelmed David. Who was he that the Father should bless him in such a way? He was just a humble shepherd, from an impure family, having married foreigners. But

David, through God's mercy and grace, was a true son of Abraham, a true child of faith.

Now today, everything was prepared and ready: drawings, plans, and supplies. There were stockpiles of gold, bronze, silver, marble, stone, timber, and fine linen. There were priests trained in every element of temple duty, and hundreds of professional musicians. And above Jerusalem, on the hill of Moriah—the hill of provision, the same hill where Abraham had offered his son to the Father—the temple would be built.

The entire nation was learning what it truly meant to worship. David had lived his entire life in preparation for this time. Soon he would leave this world behind, and with it a nation of worshipers, those who knew what it was to bring a sacrifice to the Father. They would bring more than just a token offering of an animal; they would pour out their very lives before His holy fire, to be inhabited with His life.

When the Ark had come to Jerusalem, David had placed it in a tent that was unveiled and open for the nation to see. The service of priests was replaced by the service of trained musicians who taught people to bring a different kind of sacrifice before the Father—the sacrifice of the heart through song and dance. Everyone was free to come and stand before the covenant Ark of the Father. The city itself was the holy place; the dwelling of the Father and the holy of holies was Heaven above. And they, the nation of the Father, were his priests and Levites, joined ones, continually offering up their lives night and day to live in the covenant life of the Father.

Everything was set in place and David, now advanced in years, addressed his people for the final time. The crown would pass to his son, Solomon, who would build the temple in peace and would rule over the city, Jerusalem, "the possession of peace," and this great nation, princes with God.

Because of the life of the anointed one, people could come to this city to find peace. They could come to the mountain of Moriah, to make their lives an offering, to become God's holy possession and enter into His covenant love. In this place of His counsel through the Prince of Peace, they could find His strength and provision, upon the mountain of provision. From there they could go forth, carrying with them the possession of peace—Jerusalem in their hearts—and the anointing of the Father's love.

The nations would come and worship and go forth in praise. The world would look to Jerusalem, embracing the hill of provision, and find hope.

Faith had brought them through fear into the knowledge of the Lord and into His counsel, there to find His strength in the place of provision, inside the dwelling of peace.

How wonderful it is when brethren dwell together in unity!

Having fulfilled what the Father had desired of him on earth, David entered his rest in peace, leaving this world for a much greater life.

Surely his great-great-grandmother could not have known how the Father would bless her family. Surely Rahab, rescued from a city of death, had no idea her great-great-grandson would build a city of peace and the nations of the world would come to find life through it.

 The Father loved Rahab.
The Father loved David.
The Father loves you.

CHAPTER SEVEN

Prophets of Wisdom and the City of Confusion

he old prophet stood on the hill overlooking the city; he could hardly believe this day had come. It seemed surreal, overwhelming, shocking, and horrid. Life as he had known and loved it was fading before his eyes. The great and terrible day was upon them. Looking down across the city he could remember all those years ago, when the call had first come to him. Out of Heaven a voice had spoken to him and his life had never been the same.

The young prophet drew the cord taut and with a slight tug the little lamb softly bleated and followed obediently up the hill. The lamb and his master ascended.

Pad, pad, pad, baaaaa.

Innocence veiled the lamb from the burden that he was to bear, yet the moment weighed heavily upon the boy, knowing full well the weight he was carrying. The call had come to him and he was answering it. The fear of what lay ahead made the youngster's knees quiver. The lamb, perfect in innocence, had no need to fear. He trusted his master.

Pad, pad, pad, baaaaa.

The fears of any normal young man had paled into insignificance the moment that the voice spoke to him. The message was clear; he was called as a messenger to the throne of Heaven. His choice was even clearer: either serve His master in Heaven in trembling and awe, or fear and serve man. As fearful as God is, it was a far better choice to serve One so unchanging than to serve man, who changes with the wind.

Each step now registered his choice with greater determination.

Baaaaa.

The road to the top was humbling. He cast his imagination back 300 years into the past to the glorious day when it had begun....

The weight of the Ark, the symbol of the covenant, was carried upon the shoulders of the priests, who led a procession bringing the implements of the temple up the hill. Following behind were singers, musicians, and dancers, celebrating the glorious life and love of the ever-living God. Next were the heads of states and King Solomon himself, the anointed one of Israel and David's heir.

Full of joy and wonder, they reached the top and entered the eastern gate of the temple's outer courts. They passed through to the courtyard, then the priests went ahead into the Holy Place and finally into the Most Holy Place, each new level more perfect and pure than the previous one. In the Most Holy Place, the Ark of the Covenant was laid to rest.

Sacrifices too great in number to count were offered. As the smoke of their heartfelt offerings floated into the sky, the smoke of the fire of Heaven entered the building, veiling a great ball of fire—the pure unfiltered love of God in all its glory. This love was so pure that man in his sinful state could not even look upon it, let alone stand in the midst of it; for in the fire of His glory is every aspect of love, including its justice and truth. Man, guilty under the curse of sin, could not exist in love in its purest form. He would be called immediately into account for judgment.

But the mercy of love protected him from the justice of love.

At the sight of the cloud-veiled light of life, every man was compelled, by the sin within him, to fall on his face before it. For no greatness of pride in man can stand before the greatness of God's full glory; truth compels him to fall on his face.

The temple was beautiful to behold, the stone architecture decorated in brass and lined with timber. Its implements were covered in pure gold.

Next to the temple stood the new and glorious palace of David's anointed heir and son, King Solomon, prince of peace. Solomon would rule with the justice of love, providing a degree of wisdom at which the world would marvel.

The picture was almost perfect.

God love dealt in two forms in Jerusalem. Through the ministry of the anointed high priest in the temple He offered man the peace of His merciful love. Through the ministry of the anointed king He offered man the peace of justice and expanded the dominion of the kingdom by spreading the message of the Father's just and merciful love to the world.

Justice and mercy were now married on earth in a union of love. The true glory, though, belonged to mercy, the wife of the union, whose infinite beauty was made known to the world by her husband, justice.

Just as a wife is a husband's beauty and the object of his love, she is protected and cared for by her husband. Mercy and justice were established on the mountain of Zion, meaning "fortress," for they were established by God in a place of strength and security. Below them was the mountain of provision and around them was the city of peace.

Thus the Israelites came through the possession of peace, to the place of provision and through provision into the Father's strength on the mountain of Zion. There they would find His wisdom through the rule of his prince of peace.

Mercy and justice presided over the kingdom that was established of God. Through them the world came to wonder in awe at the magnificence and beauty of God's love. The Artist of Creation had painted through redeemed man a phenomenally, wondrous, and beautiful picture of His character and amazing love.

As Solomon grew in wisdom, so the nation grew in prosperity. So great did they grow that the world came to wonder at how such a tiny nation could amass such great wealth and strength. Even the Queen of Sheba came to wonder at Solomon.

But it was only when Solomon ran out of earthly wisdom, that he came to know the Father's wisdom. It was only after conquering every challenge and acquiring every luxury, experiencing all that the world had to offer, that Solomon came to understand the greatest wisdom of man: vanity of vanities, *all* is vanity. (See Ecclesiastes 1:2.)

Vanity declares that man can accomplish nothing in this world that holds any true value, because it all fades. When you grasp this lesson, it either drives you to extinction, or it drives you to Heaven. The revelation of Heaven brings you to the true pathway of wisdom, the pathway that the wrestlers walked in the wilderness, the very starting point of God's wisdom.

The fear of Lord leads us to knowledge of the Lord, which leads us to the counsel of the Lord, which brings us to the wisdom of the Lord. In true wisdom you find that there is no other purpose but to be completely empty of yourself, that you might be full of Heaven and the life from above.

The Old and the New

It was their final day together—master and student—one leading, the other following. Elijah, the master, was a famous prophet, a wild-looking man dressed in a mantle, a cloak made of camel's hair.

The prophet's mantle was meant to be simple, uncomfortable even. It was an advertisement of the prophet's message, the true message of all prophets: to humble yourself and to seek the wisdom of Heaven.

In dark contrast, the nation had become horribly obsessed with its own glory and wisdom, and foolishly pursued the philosophies and idols of surrounding peoples. Elijah had courageously stood up to its adultery. In a confrontation on Mount Carmel, he had revealed the rudimentary nature of the machinery that drove the pagan philosophies: the idiotic and even comically foolish nature of idolatry.

The true nature of idolatry forms a philosophy of self-empowerment. It is no more than self-dressed up as God. Our desires, aspirations, and selfish motivations are embodied in a belief system that rationalizes what we do. We vainly believe that we gain power from this belief system—power to become like gods ourselves.

Not long after Elijah's time, Greek schools of philosophy were born to pursue the knowledge of idolatry. After these towers of Babel came falling down a new idol was erected—the unashamed naked pursuit of knowledge through science. Each school of thought has the same motivation dressed up in human pride: self-empowerment. The same babbling tower, erected over and over and over again, falls because it is constructed out of the pursuit of *self*.

In the midst of idolatry, Elijah came with the message that the Lord is God. His message was not just audible, it was visual. By calling both fire and rain from Heaven, he demonstrated to these "open minds" with great power that God could give life and take it away.

A Simple Mantle of Eternal Significance

His mission accomplished, he was about to be taken from this world. His student followed him, hoping to finally receive the mantle that had been offered many years ago, as he was plowing his fields. The price of the mantle was to follow Elijah to the very end, to follow the path of wisdom and to see the end result. Only then would the mantle become his.

They came to the Jordan, and Elijah placed his mantle in the river, parting the waters and bringing them through a baptism to the other side. Walking on a bit farther, Elijah was swept away by a chariot of fire, leaving Elisha and the mantle that had brought him from watery baptism to fiery baptism. Elijah was no longer on this earth.

Elisha picked up the mantle, the pathway of the prophet, and began his mission. With double the power of Elijah, Elisha, meaning *God will save,* was sent to call the nation to return to the covenant and show them that the Father could save them from their enemies. For a time, the nation obeyed God's voice.

But eventually, they returned to their idolatrous ways. Sometime after Solomon's passing, the ten tribes of the northern kingdom split from the southern kingdom. Were taken into slavery to serve their idols in the same physical chains to which their souls were bound.

Through Isaiah's Wisdom

It was a tense time for the nation. The southern kingdom had lost a great king, one who had brought reform and brought the nation back to the covenant. But with his passing, there was uncertainty as to whether his heir would carry on the same path.

The prophet Isaiah had been spending time in the Father's presence, but the presence had so enveloped the prophet that soon he found himself standing before God Himself. The living creatures were surrounding the life-giving light of God, crying His holiness, just as they surrounded it on the Ark; but their faces were veiled by their wings, and the face of the Father was veiled in a cloud of smoke.

Just like the Israelites in the desert, Isaiah was suddenly aware of his unholiness and fell on his face, crying, "Woe is me," the true fear of the Lord entering his heart. One of the angels came and brought to his lips a coal from the altar of Heaven, signifying the true sacrifice. Isaiah's lips and he himself were cleansed. Isaiah, now a possession of the Father, was sent to the nation with a mission.

Godly wisdom teaches us to give up our lives *completely,* to become a living sacrifice and to live the life of the Father. When we have accomplished this surrender, we find that we have entered into the true discernment of life: understanding.

Until we arrive at this place, the true glory of God's love is veiled from us. When we are given over to His life, we come to the place where we can see Him for who He truly is.

Isaiah saw it, or rather Him, one whose coming was a mystery. But Isaiah understood the mystery of the One who would come in fear, knowledge, counsel, strength, wisdom and understanding. This One would come from the line of David, and would be called the Anointed One. The fullness of the Father would dwell in Him. He would suffer for His people, to bring them to the covenant love of the Father, just as David had done.

This One understood that the nation would be cast off for their lack of faith and their adulterous hearts, but that a believing remnant would return, a remnant that would recognize Him when they saw Him. They would recognize Him because faith was in them and they knew the Father. They understood the Father and therefore, they would understand the Anointed One.

Baaaaa.

Young Jeremiah entered the temple courts. He loved this place even though he greatly feared its power. Sadly, the glory of the temple was fading. Years of neglect in this museum of world wonders had caused the paint to crack and fade; its gold and bronze had been stripped to pay national debt. The king sacrificed the temple to pay for protection rather than seeking the Father in the temple for protection. What remained now was mostly cold stone.

But in his heart the true glory of God's house lived on. God had called him to be a messenger of His true glory in Heaven and he was here to answer the call. Though the brick and mortar glory had faded, the Father's hadn't. A zeal and a passion for this place burned within Jeremiah.

He had come to bring a special offering before the Lord. This was not the obligatory sin offering, which the men of his country offered as a casual request for forgiveness without the real revelation that they needed it. Jeremiah was bringing a burnt offering.

He reverently approached the altar with his offering obediently in tow and laid his quivering hand upon the tender lamb's head. Less than three years old, the lamb looked back at him in innocence and, perhaps, with a sense of trepidation.

In the Father's eyes the little lamb was now the symbol of the young man's life, or more accurately his sin. With that in mind Jeremiah took the knife and separated the lifeblood of the animal from its body. The blood flowed into a bowl held by the priest.

This was not just the usual token gesture. The entire animal was placed on the altar and totally consumed by the fire, the smoke of it ascending into heaven as an offering of incense unto the Father.

But the Father took no pleasure in the death of the poor animal. The real incense was the prayer of Jeremiah's heart offered up into Heaven. Jeremiah had received a call from Heaven—a call for his entire life to be offered up to God as a vessel for His purpose. God wanted a man like Jeremiah who could weep before the Lord.

Like the prophets before him, Jeremiah would walk a road of persecution, shame, and potentially martyrdom for living the message of truth in days when the politically correct were in power.

Jeremiah, meaning *established of God,* was called not only to spread the message about the imminent destruction of Jerusalem, but also to share the good news of the future return of those who were truly established of God. He knew there would be no joy in his task, yet love overwhelmed the sorrow. Love for the Father, love for His house, love for His covenant were greater than Jeremiah's love of his own life.

The Father had asked Jeremiah to be a living offering unto Him. The innocent lamb whose smoke now burned toward Heaven was Jeremiah's unmistakable answer. Like the bride of a man doomed to die, Jeremiah offered an answer that can only come from pure love, one that makes hearts of men and women stand still: "I do."

And with that the young prophet left the temple.

He cried out from Heaven. From the heart of the Father He called for His children. From the heart of the groom He called to His bride. His message was carried upon the wind of the spirit. Searching. Searching. Searching. Searching…for a receptive ear, for someone to hear.

Now Heaven was crying. The heavenly throne room was filled with weeping. The Lord seated upon His throne was broken-hearted. His people were rejecting His love.

He called through many prophets throughout the ages, and still His Bride would not hear. She was too busy baring her soul to every idle philosophy that she could find. She had had a taste of true love but was not willing to pay the price for it. She preferred instead the cheap and nasty version.

On every hill, altar, pole, tree, or shrine she went searching…she gained the temporary pleasure of uniting her soul to another philosophy, belief or purpose—only to find afterward that she was more ravenous and hungry than before. She was hungering for food that could not satisfy, searching for that which could not quench.

The garments of her harlotry were stained with guilt. The pain within tore at her soul, but her hunger only drove her further and deeper into warping.

Every so often she would hear the voice calling from a distance. Sometimes it drove her to anger, the guilt within her searing at her lonely heart. Other times she would remember, look back upon the memories of love and return home, to her husband, to the master chambers, to meet with Him and entreat His love again.

But always…always…the incense burned in the highest places of her heart, smoldering to the sky as a silent prayer to her idols. She was never her husband's alone.

Oh how He longed for her, calling out to her continually, "Come home!"

But she ignored Him.

He sent many messengers and she killed them. He could have made her the finest maiden in the world. The nations would have marveled at her beauty as they did in Solomon's day. But now she was the joke of the nations. If her husband was so wonderful, why did she seek another?

Why do we? Our words declare our love and admiration for our King, but our hearts speak differently. Often we come to meet with Him, lay our offering at His feet and hope that He will bless us so that we can go to worship our idols again.

Often we call unto Him for His salvation, knowing secretly that we still want our own life. Often we lay ourselves before Him and beg Him to take care of us, only to go and give ourselves to other philosophies of empowerment.

But He won't, He can't. For every blessing would drive us further away, further from the truth. Every correction, no matter how gentle, would only feed our warping.

Sometimes we don't want or don't love the truth. Intimacy with the Maker of truth is far too vulnerable, too revealing, too discomforting—far too fearful.

We prefer the one-night stands and fleeting affairs with our substitutes. They don't speak back, other than to tell us what we want to hear. With them we are safe—or so we think. But where is the strength, where is the peace? Our lovers are philosophies that promise peace and prosperity, but only give pain in the end.

Love without commitment knows no such words. There is no *give* in the love of self, only *take, take, take.* Everyone throws out their bait, hoping it will land them a catch, but no one wants to let go when they get it. The love of the world couldn't be further from true love, His love—a love of eternal commitment, everlasting strength, unending peace, and gentle correction.

But true love could not wait any longer. There was only one course of action short of allowing His Bride, the nation, to completely destroy herself. He would cast her off. The one whom He had brought out of slavery and given so much of his heart to, would be cast away, for a time. He knew there was no true repentance in her. But someday there would be, at least in a remnant of her. Better to give up the illusion of love now and someday inherit a much truer love.

Jeremiah cried out from his prison cell. He had cried out for the Lord his entire life. He had given up his own pleasure in life to be a voice. And now the voice cried. The speaker of the voice had been tormented and oppressed by the hearers. Now the speaker was captive.

True love had tried to warn His Bride of this day, but she would not listen. He had called to her repeatedly, but she would not hear.

This day would come; however, if she submitted herself to it, He would be gentle.

But she would not submit. She refused to believe, refused even to listen. And the living message, the prophet of God, was locked away in a cell at the peak of his beloved city.

She thought, "Surely He will not leave us."

But the incense burned.

"Surely we are His."

Incense of idols burned on the hills.

"See how we love His bedroom, we love the temple."

In a period of revival, a revival of the temple, a darker form of idolatry was growing—the idolatry of God Himself. They had built their own image of God. A god who didn't mind their sin, who forgave it merely because they brought a sacrifice. A god who didn't care if the incense of the idols burned at the same time as the incense of the temple. A god who didn't mind sharing his bed with another.

In the most sinister form of *warping*, intimacy had been replaced with familiarity—incense burning.

But the army was upon them.

Away she was carried—to Babylon, "confusion," the nation descended from the infamous tower and the symbolic mother city of idolatry. Like a slave she was bound, shackled, carried off, paraded like a caged animal, and humiliated before men. No city could contrast more greatly to Jerusalem than Babylon.

Jerusalem: established by God and set high on a hill.
Babylon: established by man and raised up out of a swamp.

Jerusalem: a city united by a surrounding wall.
Babylon: a city divided by a river.

Jerusalem: the city where the truth
of God was glorified.
Babylon: the city where the
knowledge of man was glorified.

Jerusalem: possessor of peace.
Babylon: possessor of confusion.

To confusion we are sent as well. We think surely the Lord will not cast us off (See how we love to worship Him!), but the secret idolatry of our hearts still burns. We go to worship Him, then come home to read our own books and magazines and watch our television programs—all with the aim to empower ourselves, to achieve *our* desires and *our* purposes!

We court other philosophies and became so enthralled with them that the line between truth and fiction becomes too difficult to see, our warping too great for us to bear. In mercy He casts us off, and we go into confusion.

There upon the shores of Babylon, the Bride looked toward her home and tears welled in her eyes.

> *By the rivers of Babylon we sat and wept when we remembered Zion. There on the poplars we hung our harps, for there our captors asked us for songs, our tormentors demanded songs of joy; they said, "Sing us one of the songs of Zion!" How can we sing the songs of the Lord while in a foreign land?* (Psalm 137:1-4)

Jeremiah now stood a free man, to gaze upon his beloved city, Jerusalem, while the Lord's Bride was gone in chains. He looked upon the streets that once were filled with mirth, the homes that once were warm with fires. But the smoke smoldering up from the rubble was all that remained of his glorious city. And the temple lay in ruins; the presence of the true love was gone.

And Heaven wept, the tears flowing down Jeremiah's face and onto his breast before puddling on the cold stone at his feet. Heaven wept bitterly. True love longed to hold His Bride, longing to gather her to Himself like a mother hen does her chicks. But she would not have Him.

But someday, someday…the anointed One of David would come. The Lord would rescue His Bride, and bring her to His home. There He will wipe away every stain and tear and every bit of dirt and she would be clean, holy to him again. She will clothe herself in white and they will stand together before the world to renew their vows, with a greater marriage covenant than before. And she will be new.

Jeremiah looked toward heaven and reminded himself of true love and the memories that they shared. His heart rang out the cry of the Bride—and the cry of my own heart: *Come, Lord.*

CHAPTER EIGHT

The Son

He ascended the hill of Jerusalem, the old man, humbly climbing toward the proud temple that now crowned the top of the rebuilt city, a city that had seen many tears since the years of Solomon and the days of Jeremiah.

The turmoil had weighed heavily upon the people. Many tyrannical leaders had held the cities reins tightly, milking it for their own glory and satisfaction.

The feeble, gray-haired man reached the temple mount and wedged through crowds of worshipers, most of them well dressed in long, flowing robes and spewing long-winded prayers.

Much of the idolatry common to early Israel had slipped away, but the spirit behind it now lived on in an even more sinister fashion—religious pride.

The temple courts were filled with those who had made an image in their minds of a god who looked vaguely like the One the Scriptures spoke of. Inwardly this god was only a reflection of their own selfish desires.

Regularly they came to the courts to bring a sacrifice and call out to God for the return of their kingdom. The incense rose skyward from their sin offerings, but not toward Heaven. The incense was for their own pleasure, to veil the true nature of their desires as they stood in the temple courts to platform their political aims and financial power. They made profits on the sale of animals for sacrifice; there were money changing tables and clandestine meetings with other profit-minded people.

It was big business, a circus of great entertainment and self-promotion, all under the guise of God's Kingdom. Overlooking this busy financial district was the new palace and in it the pseudo-king of Israel. With him they bore a love-hate relationship. Their Saul, Herod, *their hero,* had built their magnificent temple and city, but at a high price—the nation's soul was his.

Overlooking this great plaza Herod pulled the strings of power, wielding the mighty weight of the Roman Empire, the new Babylon. He took the finest of spoils and beauty for himself. The people hated their slavery to Herod, though not enough to give up their own power and success, the pursuits of their own lives.

Amidst this pretense of worship and crying to God, the lowly old servant quietly made his way toward the inner courts of the temple. He had come in obedience to the same voice that had spoken to Jeremiah, David, Joshua, Moses, Abraham, and even to Adam—hoping beyond hope that today his aging eyes would behold what he had longed after for so many years.

The light was growing dim as the sun was setting on his life. There was nothing for him personally to gain from the coming of the Anointed One—the *Messiah* in his language and *Christ* in the Greek. He came not for himself but with hope in his soul for the generations to follow.

"There," the voice of Heaven nudged him.

Pushing through the crowd was a young woman, clutching a tiny newborn child under the gentle yet watchful eye of her husband. This child was Him, the one promised to Eve. He had been born of a virgin by the very seed of God—the One who would be bruised by the serpent for man's redemption.

The worshipers paid almost no attention to the unassuming parents or their helpless little child, but the fading eyes of an old man saw more clearly than anyone else in the temple—here was the salvation that they cried out for, but would not see. Their warped image of God blinded them to the real image of God, even in their very midst.

Like Simeon, only those who listen with ears of faith will see with their eyes the promises they hope for. *Simeon* means, "he listens."

Crack!

The whip striped across His back, driving him closer to the end of three years of earthly ministry. He was hours away from finishing what He had come to do. It was the greatest moment in the history of the world.

In the beginning were the Father and the Son. Together they created the world and painted the sky—one directing, the other acting. Together they formed a symphony, harmony upon melody. A moving concert. A blissful partnership. Nothing revealing the

Father's heart of love more than the fact that He chose to bring forth all of creation through the hands of His Son.

The Father was the painter, the Son the brush. The Father was the craftsman; the Son the tools. The Father was the sculptor, the Son his hands. The Father was the voice; the Son the light that came from the voice.

The Son was the living message of the Father to creation; how the Father revealed his personality of love and perfect life, through everything that was made.

The Son—the light of the world!

Crack!

The Son was riveted in anguish as the whip again tore flesh from His already raw back. He came to earth as a mere man, flesh and blood, calling Himself nothing more than the Son of Man.

But man's image and name had been warped on the earth. Just like the serpent, the father of the sinful, man was responsible for propagating sin, death, and deception across the planet. Everything given into his dominion suffered because of it: sea, land, air, fish, plants, birds, mammals, and children—all suffered under the curse of death brought by man's warped image. And now the Son had taken that name and its reputation upon Himself: to sleep, eat, drink, think, weep, live, and die as a man.

Why? Why assume that image?

As a common man He had come to meet people where they were, in the place where they lived, to restore them, to bring them to the life and purpose that the Father had for them from the beginning: to be the image of the Father.

Man himself was made to be a living message of God. Created in His image, man was meant to reflect Father and Son; that reflection was to bring life out of darkness, order out of chaos, beauty out of blandness, love out of selfishness. Just like the first Adam, created in the image and beauty of the Father, the second Adam—the Son—came as a humble man to restore mankind to that same image of the Father.

What was that image?

Perfect selfless love, just like the Father's. Not seeking the love of self, but seeking to give life to others. The very nature and image of the Father of creation was the reason He chose to save man through the Son.

Crack!

The whip drove Him on.

The Son had called out to them to leave everything behind, and they had. They had left businesses, homes, family, friends, and reputations—all of it. To many their choice seemed extreme; no, worse—lunacy. Why leave behind wealth and comforts to follow a man who had no army, no wealth, no land, no city, no nation, not even a great name? It was extreme.

But the Son was unapologetic. This was the price to pay for following in His footsteps. Why? Because it was the price the Son was paying.

But why demand such a price? What sort of love would ask you to give up all of that? The kind of love that provided so much more.

The Son came to offer them the love of the Father: a love that desired to fill them with peace beyond comprehension, wealth beyond understanding and time beyond measure. The Son came to give them life abundantly. But love and life are received by faith: we trust in love to fulfill its promises to bring us to life.

137

Abraham learned this lesson and became the father of a great nation. Now the Father of creation was asking them to abandon a nation on earth, for a nation so much greater and a city so much more beautiful. He was offering them a place in his own home—Heaven itself.

But to walk this sort of faith, to follow after something they couldn't see, feel, or touch meant giving up all that they knew to journey to a land yet unseen, just like Abraham.

Many were clutching dearly to the possessions of earth. They found comfort in the things they owned. Some loved themselves and all their possessions so much that they were terrified to let go of the trinkets and earthly junk to lay hold of the vast wealth of Heaven.

They were too afraid to trust in the love of the Father. Though they called themselves the children of Abraham, yet few had the faith of Abraham; few were worthy to be called children of faith.

Yet the Father, knowing that this kind of faith was difficult for them, had sent the Son—the promised seed of Abraham. Abraham went before the nation to show by his life the journey of the faithful to the Promised Land. The Son would go before the nation to show by His life the journey of the faithful to eternal life.

Now the Son, obeying His father unto death, was exemplifying the truth that love is stronger than death.

The Voice

The voice cried out from the wilderness, "Prepare the way of the Lord!"

He was the last of the voices of the old way, a prophet in the spirit of Elijah complete with the humble, camel-hair cloak and a health-food diet of locusts and wild honey. His name was *John,* meaning "God is giving-love," and his voice carried the purpose of the Father's entire message from the fall of man in the Garden until now—to prepare the coming of the Lord on earth.

John's message was the same as that of Moses, who prepared the Israelites to leave their bondage to meet with the Father in the wilderness. John stood at the bank of the descending river calling to those who had ventured into the wilderness. He urged them to hear his simple message, leave behind their old ways, and be born again into the new, coming life of the promised One.

"Prepare the way of the Lord," the voice called out.

Splash!

Bare feet stepped into the water, human feet that walked the path of humanity, wading deeper and deeper into the cool flow of death until He was completely submerged.

Following in the footsteps of Moses, *The One Pulled from the Water* came to lead them through baptism, to bring them to the covenant mountain and from there, to the Father's house. He didn't enter the baptism waters for His own life, just as He didn't enter this world for Himself, but for those watching. For them "For them, he was a living tabernacle, demonstrating—like the Levites glowing in the light of the brass bath in the wilderness— the glorious life of sonship that awaits for those who offer their lives to the Father in faith —like the Levites entering the brass bath in the wilderness—the glorious life of sonship that awaits those who offer their lives to the Father in faith.

As the Son stepped out from the river, the glory of the Father shown on Him, and the Spirit of His love came on Him. Like a dove, the symbol of peace, the Spirit brought the anointing from Heaven to Him…the anointing to bring peace.

And the voice of the Father spoke, "This is My *beloved* Son in whom I am well pleased."

✦ Teaching the Way ✦

Many had followed the Son to the wilderness and to the mountain. There they waited for the Son to come and teach them, like the Israelites had waited for Moses in the wilderness.

They were hungry—not just physically, but spiritually—desiring the strength and nourishment of Heaven, the nourishment of intimacy with God. But this was not a mountain of fear as Sinai had been. Those standing on the mountain already feared God and desired to enter into knowing Him. They had demonstrated their fear by entering into John's baptism at the Jordan.

The feet of their mediator descended from the summit of the mountain to teach them, like Moses, bringing them the commandments of a new covenant agreement. The Son called forward from among them 12 who would be leaders in a new kingdom. He instructed first the 12, then the others. This disorganized group of followers would eventually be reorganized around this group of 12—though unlike the earthly tribe and family of their desert forefathers, this would be a heavenly family.

Contrary, however, to their popular opinion, the Son hadn't come to abolish the law, but to fulfill its purpose by writing it on their hearts; to show them what the law truly meant. The Father had purposed through the law to create a society where covenant love would be modeled. The law was given to teach them what love meant—to live in the life of the Father and to give life to others—and the fear that comes from knowing the cost of stepping beyond love's boundaries, the cost of death.

The nation had grown up and the Son was replacing their house rules with the real rule of love, much stricter than the Law of Moses, going far beyond actions, right to the core of who they were. Adultery, murder, divorce, all started in the heart.

The Law of Love

Only the Father's love could empower them to live in such sinless perfection. Only by giving up everything that they had, to live in complete dependence on His love, would they be free enough to love others as He commanded them. Thus the law brings us captive to love. When we see the Father's perfect standard of love, only a proud fool would try to live in this standard without first seeking God's strength to enable them to do so.

Following this love is a journey of faith. Many give up, like the rich young ruler who asked the Son what he must do to inherit eternal life. The answer, selfless love, was too great for him to follow. Had he come first thirsting and hungering after the Father's love; had he pursued this love first, nothing would have been impossible.

The standard of love is no joke. The Father is serious when He commands us to follow it. But God will not ask us to accomplish that for which He does not fill us with life and power.

Thus, the Son came to show us what it is like to follow the Father in this type of selfless love. He became for us a high priest of a new order, showing us all how to enter into the covenant life with the Father, just like He did. He was a true Levite, joined with the Father, dwelling in the Father's love and empowered by it to live His life.

The Son went far beyond teaching. He lived and breathed the true law of Moses for all to see. He lived to show us what it truly means to give our lives to the Father. He brought us into that dwelling place where we find His strength. He brought us to the table in the Father's house and gave us the bread of Heaven.

As a testimony of the covenant, Moses gave the stone tablets, written by the finger of God, but by the legacy of His life the Son gave us a personal testimony of the true and perfect covenant.

The tablets of the law were a message of covenant love, and the covenant was a message of the Father's love. The life of the Son is a greater living message of covenant love, a living message of the Father's perfect love.

Moses had ascended the mountain to make a covenant for the nation, to show to them the glorious life that awaited them when they would fully give up their lives to find the Father's life. Now, on top of another mountain, the Son's life was about to be poured out and offered to the people on the Father's behalf

Crack!

He had brought them to a spiritual Gilgal, their sin rolled away because they had put their faith in the Father's love. He had brought them to a spiritual circumcision, greater than the circumcision of Abraham, because this one cut their hearts.

Though many battles of faith lay ahead, in the Father's eyes they were clean and holy and worthy of entering into His spiritual dwelling, the true Promised Land. Here the new spiritual Joshua— or *Jesus* in Greek—counseled them to come to the table of intimacy with the Father by prayer and fasting. Through intimacy with the Father they could have strength to deliver others from sickness and disease brought by the demonic giants that possessed the land and oppressed the people. Now those who hungered for love and life, the lonely Rahabs desperate for hope, could come into the house of the Father.

Crack!

He had brought them to the homes of the poor and the sick, the reputable and the disreputable, and had taught them to carry the good news of the Kingdom of God to a desperate and needy people. Many of the people were tired of the Roman occupation, tired of the abusive tax policies, tired of being treated like second class citizens because they did not bear Roman citizenship. They were tired of temple worship that, though glamorous and polished, was empty of power to change life and to bring the one thing that they thirsted for in this spiritual famine—peace.

Through this time the students had followed their teacher and watched His hands heal and His words bring life. They saw the love of the Father in action, in power, through the Son, bringing life to all: blind men, cripples, lepers, and hedonists! One touch and they were whole—their ailments cleansed, their sins forgiven.

Blind Bartimaeus stood at the gates, wearing a beggar's robe. He had heard about the Son and the works of compassion that flowed from His hands. He was desperate for that sort of life, willing to give up anything for it—easy because he owned nothing. But his real torment was not his blind eyes, but the searing pain in his heart. From boyhood he had been told that his blindness was a curse, a punishment for sin. In a world of proud self-righteousness, no social standing was given to one with such a mark.

But though he could not see, he could hear…and believe. He heard the stories of the Son, and the power of love in His hands. He heard that the lame walked, the blind saw, and that sins were forgiven. So that day as he heard the Son passing, the desperation in his soul cried out for life! He would not be hushed. He had no pride to protect.

"Jesus! Son of David! Jesus! Have mercy on me!" His eyes could not see, and he cried out for sight…true sight to see the light of the Father's love—to find forgiveness for his brokenness and sin. It was for people like Bartimaeus that the Son had come. The nation was full of men who had only their natural eyes to navigate life; because of their spiritual blindness, they were the truly hopeless beggars. Those who knew they were blind, who were willing to strip themselves of the beggars' robes given them by idolatrous religion, could now don the robes of love.

"He's coming for you," were the beloved words that entered his ears and filled his spiritual eyes with hope. These words fed the faith within him, lifted him to his feet, drove him to cast off his beggar's robes, and gave him hope that his encounter with the Son would be the end of his misery and the beginning of life!

New eyes looked into the eyes of the Son glowing with pure and perfect love—Bartimaeus' first sight. He was a blessed man; much more than that; Bartimaeus—a *highly prized son,* as his name means—had had his sins forgiven. He was shining in the new life of the Father.

Crack!

His students now watched from a distance as their Anointed One climbed the hill, bearing the cross beam upon His shoulders.

Among the crowd, Mary Magdalene was weeping. He had come to her as a knight in shining armor, banishing demons that had tormented her soul with their taunting lies, day and night without rest. She was a woman of the world, of poor reputation, a symbolic daughter of Rahab, and she longed to be rescued, longed for true love. In Him she found it. He rescued her, set her free. Filled her with life. He wanted her heart, her true life, not just her body as other men; and for her life, He was giving up His life.

Many others in the crowd that had gathered had refused His message; many didn't want this type of leadership or His type of kingdom. Humble humanity? They wanted a leadership surrounded by great power and glory. They were content with the things of Rome, the lifestyle, culture, money, and their beloved temple, an idolatrous tribute to Rome in the name of another god. They wanted a Saul.

But the Son of David didn't care about their backgrounds or what they looked like, what people thought about them, or how successful they were. He had come to teach them about true success and prosperity—the success and prosperity of Heaven. The pathway of anointing was the heart of worship, like Mary's. This Mary had poured out upon Him a jar of anointing oil, fine perfume, costing her a year's wages. She understood that pouring her life out upon the Lord was the greatest act of worship, bringing to her a more fragrant anointing of love than her perfume could afford.

These mighty men and women were learning to use worship as a weapon. Before the Father, they poured out their lives to feed the hungry, clothe the naked, and bind up the brokenhearted. As they continually emptied their lives for others, they were continually filled with a greater, more fragrant, life from Heaven, from Him. This was worship, and it was much more than a song and a dance, or an animal on the altar. This was the way of David's mighty men, living in covenant life together.

True Love Revealed

The intimacy of the evening had made some of them uncomfortable. The hands that had touched the sick and the sinners, the perfect hands of the Son, were now touching the feet of his faithful 12 students. Having followed Him faithfully on the road, they were growing daily in the revelation of who their teacher really was. But at times it was a difficult road to walk, and many of them stumbled.

Peter, one of the leaders of the group, could remember when five thousand people were fed with five small loaves of bread and two fish, multiplied by the prayer of the Son. But when the Son challenged the crowd to seek the nourishment that came from intimacy with Him, the light of truth sent many of them scattering. The 12 sat in silence, looking depressed and desolate.

"Do you want to leave?" Jesus finally asked them.

They didn't immediately answer, probably wondering where they would go. They had given up everything to follow the Anointed One, believing that they would help usher in the new kingdom. But now, there was nowhere. Could they go to the synagogues? To the temple? No, those were dead, empty places. Finally Peter plucked up the courage to speak out the only answer, "Where else can we go? Only Your words have life."

And now Jesus was about to wash Peter's feet. Peter had worked so hard to find favor with the Son. Except for a few mistakes under his belt, he was sure that the Son was pleased with his performance. But now, the Son was about to wash Peter's feet.

This couldn't be right. Jesus was their teacher, they His students. It was not right for the teacher to take the lowliest place in the house and wash their feet. That place was reserved for the least of the servants! They had worked so hard to put their best foot forward, and now He wanted to wash and caress these ugly, smelly, tired feet!

Peter protested.

"Unless I wash your feet, you have no part of Me," Jesus replied. As the living tabernacle, He was about to bring them into the dwelling place with the Father, showing them that, like the Levites, they had to continually wash away the dirt of the world, to enter in with clean hearts. This wasn't a full baptism, but a life of continual repentance. The Son was so full of love for them that, with no concern for Himself, He was taking the place of dishonor to bring them into the dwelling place of the Father.

But this time, He would show them how to go deeper into the dwelling place than they had ever gone. He would show them how to enter into the Most Holy Place. Here inside the dwelling place, at the table of fellowship, He would nourish and strengthen them with His intimate counsel.

The Son picked up the simple bread from the table and broke it, saying, "This is My body, broken for you." Then he picked up the cup—a cup of wine poured but never drunk, a cup that belonged to Elijah. This cup signified a time when a prophet would come in the spirit of Elijah, clothed in humble humanity, to make a new covenant written on their hearts. And Christ, the One who had come in the spirit of Elijah, offered the cup of as a symbol of His blood, His very life.

By the life that He lived in the flesh, He nourished them with truth, bringing them into the place of dwelling with the Father. His own blood was about to be shed. On their behalf, He would soon make a covenant between them and the Father, so that they might receive, through Him, the life of the Father.

The Master, Teacher, and King made Himself their brother in covenant. He had taken their lives upon Himself and given His life for them. His body and His blood, every moment that He lived, were a living testimony of this covenant. He had shown them what perfect love was, and by His perfect love had taught them how to dwell with the Father, in the Father's perfect love, in the Father's possession of peace.

They were beginning to understand that the Son was much more than just the Anointed One of David; He was the very Son of God, the perfect living message of the Father's love.

This message was quite simply that God is light, the source of all life—and that those who would walk in covenant friendship with God must walk in this perfect light. Religion would seek to gray the message, to replace the light of God's love with something less pure and less demanding, something that left room for darkness. The Son had courageously shone the light in them, so there was no room left for darkness.

The Son explained to them that He was going to lead them directly to the light. They would watch as He placed Himself completely in the fire of the Father's altar, to die and ascend into Heaven, as incense, to be with the Father. He was showing them the ancient pathway of Abraham, Moses, David, Elijah—to lay down life fully; to enter into the fire of perfect dwelling with the Father; to become a living, burning offering so that others might live.

Quite simply, if they were going to be His disciples, if they were going to dwell in His kingdom, if they were going to love Him and love the Father, then they had but one commandment to follow. That was to *love one another,* as He had loved them. This path would lead them to perfect love of laying down their lives for each other, as He was about to do for them.

They were struggling to understand. They had seen the strength and power of life in Him. Why walk now in such weakness? Why die? They had yet to come to the wisdom and understanding of the prophets; they had yet to see the life that awaited them beyond the veil. And the Son knew this. He knew that only after they had watched the Son offer Himself up to the Father; only after they saw Him consumed by the fire of the Father's judgment for them, only after they became completely aware of their true sin and unholiness, their need for the cleansing coal from the altar—only then would the warping and confusion of their hearts be truly burned away and replaced by the wisdom and understanding of God.

But now they couldn't understand; no, not yet.

The Son led the 12, His covenant brothers, to the Garden of the Olive Press on the Mount of Olives. Only that morning had they stood with Him on this mountain and watched as He wept, the tears of Jeremiah pouring out of the heart of David. He wept over a city that would not receive His message. A city that would be destroyed because of its warping, because it would not reject the things of Babylon. By rejecting the truth and the true possession of peace, Jerusalem had become a city of confusion.

And now the Son was bringing the faithful remnant out of the city to the mountain and garden of anointing, where His soul was being pressed in prayer for them. He was being poured out to produce a spiritual anointing of love, far greater than that which anointed the beloved David, and to lead them to the true possession of peace, the New Jerusalem.

For them, He was going to take on the disdain and dishonor of a criminal execution—the charge: treason. It was not for His treason against Rome, but for but theirs against the Father.

And with a betrayer's kiss, the Son was led away.

Crack!

Ascending the hill of death, the Son of God spilled His own blood to make a pathway of life for the new Ark of the Covenant and those who followed, to enter into a new city. A city greater than

David, or Abraham, had ever imagined. An impenetrable New Jerusalem. A possession of eternal peace for all who dwelt in it. A city that could only be seen with spiritual eyes. Though His students could not yet see the city, they followed the Anointed One, the Messiah, the Christ. When their eyes were opened, they would behold, as a blind man gaining sight, the beauty and wonder of the life for which they longed.

In confusion and sorrow some of the 12 were watching on the distant hill with Mary.

The reason he came

"Lord, if You had been here, my brother would not have died," Mary had said only days before.

But the Son already knew. He knew without being told. He knew the grief. He knew the disappointment. He knew His friend was gone. Lazarus, one of His closest friends was dead.

Mary's eyes looked at the Savior with intense disappointment. She knew that He had the power to heal the sick. She had seen it. But this went beyond sickness; her brother was dead and her friend was too late.

But the Son knew more. He knew it was for a moment. He knew that power beyond death had been given to Him; indeed, the very power to *give* life, not just *repair* it. That moment, that time had been engineered for a purpose, engineered so that they would see love stronger than death.

"Where is He?" The living message was brought to the tomb of death, and for a moment, He was overwhelmed.

Jesus wept.

Why did the Son weep? Why did the Son weep when He knew that life would be restored? In a moment, He would embrace His dear friend again and rejoice in life. Who would mourn the loss of something that would be returned? Who would weep at that which had been lost, but was now found?

For a moment, the curtain was pulled back, to reveal it all, to reveal the reason. Four thousand years were required to prepare for this time in history when the Son would step into the world for a moment, then leave. Why He would come and face the agonizing pain of His own death?

The revealed answer: The Son wept the tears of the Father, tears of bitter grief at the pain of death and the eternity of separation from the ones He loves, from those He calls friends.

Mary believed that she would see her brother at the end of time. The Son wanted to show her, those watching, you, me, and everyone who ever reads about this story—that life is for today.

The Father sent his Son to show the world, not just that He had power to *give* life, but that He *is* life. That by knowing Him, walking as He walks, talking as He talks, living as He lives, we find life, not just some day, but immediately. Now. Today!

For He, who is the perfect picture of the Father, *is* the resurrection and the life. He doesn't just lead us to it—He *is* it.

The Moment of Truth

"Lazarus, come forth," spoke the Son, the living message of life.

Lazarus, whose name means, "God has helped," stepped out of death and into life.

Crack! Crack!

The Son reached the top of the hill—His body near exhaustion and nearing death's doorstep. He was placed across two beams. Other hands stretched His, tied down and then pierced through them with swinging blows from a hammer—painfully connecting Him to the rough wood of truth.

His body ached beyond measure. Death was preying upon Him. The cross was hoisted into the air and sunk into a hole. In this moment the whole world and all of history would be seen in one clear moment of truth—not *a* truth, not a *form* of truth, but truth at its roots.

The word *truth* means "strength," and is derived from the English word *tree*. Thus the *tree of truth* was telling the story of truth. The cross was planted on the hill of the skull, stretching both upward and downward, representing the connection of the truth of God to the mind of man. In this moment the truth of Heaven was brought to earth in His perfect plan.

The Son of Man, the One sent from Heaven, was hanging on the cross, representing perfect, selfless love. The perfect love that only comes from Heaven was made human, to bring the truth of Heaven to us, to renew our minds and to redeem our lives.

But sin was also present, represented by two thieves, one hanging, dying, on either side, like all of us. The one to His left represents those who through unbelief reject His love, mocking the truth: "You can't even save yourself." The world looks down upon those who surrender themselves to the love of the Father and mocks their weakness and selfless love.

The other thief, who stood up for the truth, represented the righteous, who are made righteous only because they accept and come to love the truth. To them is given the promise that they will enter into the Kingdom of Heaven. How amazing that a thief on a cross could see what the religious leaders could not: that among them was far more than a man. He was the Son of God Himself.

Thus the cross brings judgment to all based on how we receive it. When you face Christ with His hands and arms open, you see the truth and love of God stripped naked and made shameful by the sin of the world. You either reject it as lunacy or you accept at as the greatest, purest act of love that the world has ever seen. Either way, everyone faces the cross of truth and answers the question in his own heart.

It is a perfect picture of both the love of God and the cost of sin. The Son came not to judge but to offer His life. Yet we are judged by how we receive it, because we judge ourselves.

This was and is the serpent's greatest victory and greatest defeat in one moment. On one hand, those who embrace the truth of the cross, embrace the Kingdom of Heaven and find victory over death. On the other hand, its judgment forces those who hate the truth to reject it and embrace fully the kingdom of hell. In seeking to kill the Son, they had purposely sought to destroy the truth. No longer could satan hide in the murky waters of ignorance. The truth was shining and dividing the world in two—Heaven and hell, life and death, dark and light, true colors showing.

The Worst Was Yet to Come

The Son was about to undergo a baptism of fire—the fire that gave birth to hell itself. He took upon Himself all of the judgment, the death, and destruction that the Father had stored for those who rejected His love. The Son had taken upon Himself the sin and death of His covenant brothers, of the tax collectors, of the harlots, of the world—and for them He would experience the judgment of the Father.

The judgment was made far worse because He had never been separated from the Father by sin. He had always lived in perfect fear of the Father, looking into His eyes, with the same pure innocence of a little baby looking into the eyes of a loving father, with complete and perfect trust.

The fire fell.
The Son screamed.
The Father wept.
The earth shook, violently.

Those who looked upon Him wondered in great fear: "Surely this must be the Son of God." Truth shone brightly.

Then, all was silent.

"It is finished," said the Son brokenly and He breathed His last breath.

A New Day Dawns

In the early morning she came to the tomb to properly anoint the body for burial. He had been her entire source of life. Mary Magdalene had followed Him nearly everywhere. On the day He died she was the last to leave Him; now she was the first to return to the tomb. He had been her life and her soul. She had given herself to Him completely, trusting in Him to lead her to life. Now He was gone. It was over. At least she could anoint His body for death as He had anointed the death of her soul with His life.

But finding the tomb empty was too much. Her sorrow overwhelmed her and her eyes welled with tears. She couldn't even anoint His body. It was gone.

"Why are you weeping?" said a voice softly.

Was this the man who had taken His body away? Would he know where her master was?

"Sir, if you have taken Him, please tell me where He is."

"Mary," said a voice she recognized, a voice that spoke deep into her soul, touching her where no physical touch could reach. She knew Him. The realization dawned in her mind, not by His appearance, but by His voice. Three days ago, with unbearable grief, she had cried out for this voice—a voice she longed to hear speak hope into her heart again, the voice of life!

"My Master!" she cried, tears flowing from an invisible fountain of joy. She was safe in His love, a love would that would never be taken away from her again. Ever.

His followers gathered at the top of the mountain, the Mountain of Olives. Some came because they had heard a rumor, others came because it was real—they had seen, touched, spoken to Him. Among them were the 12.

At His request, they stood with Him on the peak of the mountain. Having died to this world and suffered the wrath of the Father, He was now again alive because of the Father's love.

Not only was He alive—He was now living in a body that could never die, a body no longer subject to the laws of this world, the laws of death and the power of sin. He was free.

After His resurrection, the Son met with His disciples, now short of Judas the betrayer, and explained to them what they had seen, having watched Him pass through death, as a sacrifice upon the altar, into the Most Holy Place with the Father. They had died with Him, their hearts completely joined to Him in love, and they had arisen with Him, becoming alive to the wisdom and understanding of Heaven.

He had become the example for them of what lay ahead: life, eternal, unlimited life. And in His life, they would live because they knew Him. He lived for them, and, as He had been, they were in a period of transition from death unto life. One day, they too would be completely free from the laws of this world and would live fully to the laws of Heaven. One day love would be perfected in them.

The full anointing of love dwelt in the Son: fear and knowledge, counsel and strength, wisdom and understanding, all of these leading to truth, the fullness of the other six. The sevenfold spirit of love burned with life, shining within the Son like the candlestick in the tabernacle.

As He had dwelt with them in body, soon He would dwell with them in another way. His Spirit, the Spirit of truth, would come and fill them with the life that the Son had lived in, teaching and guiding them by the love of the Father. They would know His power to overcome the world. The Spirit would bring them the source of life itself, beyond the veil, just as the Son had known.

As they learned to live together in the love that the Son had taught them, the Spirit, the anointing from Heaven, came and lived within them, bringing Heaven to them. And there they dwelt in the love of the Father. The Spirit is also our advocate. He guides us, instructs and even fights for us. The Spirit teaches us the way to fullness of life with the Father.

As the Son finished teaching and began to ascend toward Heaven like incense from the altar, He was joined by a cloud of witnesses who had, by faith, come to the same altar, completely surrendered to the Father. This cloud stands between us and the fire of life at the center of the universe, beckoning us to come and join them.

For us, who answer their call, there awaits a journey of faith, a path made straight by the life of the Son into the everlasting life of the Father.

Until we meet in the arms of the Father...

> *The Spirit of the Lord will rest on Him—the Spirit of wisdom and of understanding, the Spirit of counsel and of power, the Spirit of knowledge and of the fear of the Lord* (Isaiah 11:2).

> *And I will ask the Father, and He will give you another Counselor to be with you forever—the Spirit of truth* (John 14:16-17a).

Looking for the next step?

Visit:
www.followtheancientpath.com

To contact us by e-mail:
info@followtheancientpath.com

Want to know more about the author?

Visit:
www.joshuajost.com

Additional copies of this book and other book titles from DESTINY IMAGE EUROPE are available at your local bookstore.

We are adding new titles every month!

To view our complete catalog on-line, visit us at:
www.eurodestinyimage.com

Send a request for a catalog to:

Via Acquacorrente, 6
65123 - Pescara - ITALY
Tel. +39 085 4716623 - Fax +39 085 4716622

"Changing the world, one book at a time."

Are you an author?

Do you have a "today" God-given message?

CONTACT US

We will be happy to review your manuscript for a possible publishing:

publisher@eurodestinyimage.com